SCHOOL DEVELOPMENT PLANNING

by

Brent Davies and Linda Ellison

LONGMAN

Published by Longman Industry and Public Services
Management, Longman Group UK Ltd, 6th Floor, Westgate
House, The High, Harlow, Essex CM20 1YR
Telephone: Harlow (0279) 442601; Fax: Harlow (0279) 444501;
Telex: 81491 Padlog

© Longman Group UK Ltd 1992

A catalogue record for this book is available from the British
Library

ISBN 0-582-08179-3

Typeset by Communitype Communications Ltd, Leicester
Printed and bound by Bell and Bain Ltd, Glasgow

Contents

Dedication

This book is dedicated to the staff of the Bexley Directorate of Education and the headteachers of Bexley schools.

Preface

The rapid changes that have followed the 1988 *Education Reform Act* have involved schools in introducing the National Curriculum, standardised assessment and testing, Local Management of Schools (LMS) and Grant Maintained Status (GMS). While coping with and meeting the challenge of any of the individual reforms in itself seems difficult, coping with them all within a limited time frame presents a major management challenge for a school.

These changes have been combined with the overall shift in the relationship between central government, local education authorities (LEAs) and individual schools. With the polarisation of the system putting more power in the hands of central government and in the hands of individual schools at the expense of LEAs, a fresh look has to be taken at management at the institutional level. The advent of decentralised school management has placed at school level the responsibility to undertake the coordinated planning of educational provision. This means that schools have to provide integrated plans for their activities that not only include the traditional planning responsibilities but also many new ones that they took over from the LEA when they adopted full LMS or GM status.

Planning for an educational institution in this new era of decentralised school management calls for an integration of all aspects of a school's activities and the planning of them not only for the following year but also over a medium term perspective of a three year period. With the rapid changes in the education system, planning cannot be a precise activity but the very nature of a changing environment calls for a structured planning framework within which to adjust to changed circumstances.

This book sets out to provide the guidance necessary to enable schools to undertake the major elements within the school development planning process. It takes the reader through a discussion of the nature and dimensions of planning followed by an examination of the cycle of activity that is needed in order to create a plan. The detailed elements of a school development plan are examined with a consideration of the role of the individuals involved in the process. The book puts forward an outline format for a school development plan and applies it to case studies of a primary and a secondary school to demonstrate the application of the approach. The authors hope that readers will find this of practical assistance when designing and completing their own school development plans.

Acknowledgements

We would like to acknowledge a number of people and organisations for their help and assistance in developing the ideas and material contained in this book: Les Bettinson (ex Stockport LEA) for testing our initial ideas on school development plans; Martin Morris, the headteacher of Bacup and Rawtenstall Grammar School, for the use of the school development plan audit material; Newton Thompson, the headteacher of New Parks Community College, for the use of part of the college development plan; John Cain and Helen Gunter for help with the Secondary Case Study; and especially the help and support of the staff of the Directorate of Education and headteachers of the London Borough of Bexley for many aspects of the book — in particular for their innovative school development plan reporting format. We would, finally, like to thank Hazel Davies for her help in producing the book.

THOSE WHO DO NOT PLAN

PLAN TO FAIL

1 The nature and dimensions of school development planning

Local Management of Schools (LMS) and Grant Maintained Status (GMS) have focused attention on the need for effective planning at the school level. The thrust of the 1988 *Education Reform Act*, which introduced these changes, was to enable schools to be self-managing institutions determining how their resources can be used to deliver an effective curriculum. School managers, therefore, have the key task of planning how their institution is to adapt and change to meet the challenge of providing effective education for pupils and students in the 1990s. The quality of management planning will be one of the critical determinants of a school's success.

The danger that is inherent in the move to decentralised school management is that budgeting is seen as *the* most important activity. It is most important that finance should be seen as neither the starting point nor as a separate activity from the education process; it is simply the facilitator of the education process. If schools are to develop and further their educational mission, finance should be seen in the context of what the school is trying to achieve and not as predetermining the debate on curriculum. In order to achieve this, a school needs an integrated development plan which takes a longer term view of needs and their resourcing than has been the case in the past.

School development planning enables those who govern to

concentrate on policies and those who manage to manage effectively; it combines the energies of governors and managers in searching for greater effectiveness, efficiency and community satisfaction. It is this approach which has to be adopted to meet the needs of schools as increasingly self-governing institutions. The major concern is that, bearing in mind the available resources, an effective education must be provided for all pupils. To do this governors and staff should work together to prepare and carry out a development plan for the school. This needs to project the school forward over a three year period so that change is anticipated and successfully managed. The school development plan should encompass all aspects of the school's life, integrating plans for different areas of school activities.

The purpose of this book is to assist schools in the process of development planning. While the term used is *development* it is vitally important that schools use the plan to concentrate on the main task of efficiently and effectively managing *existing provision* as well as giving attention to changes and developments.

This chapter is structured into two main sections to assist schools in reflecting on their own school development plans. The first section reviews the general nature of planning. The second one sets out to answer some very practical questions about the nature and purpose of school development plans before the book moves on, in Chapter Two, to examine the process of school development planning.

General nature of planning

Planning is the managerial process of deciding in advance *what* is to be done and *how* it is to be done. More specifically, we interpret planning to be the broad process of determining the school's direction, translating this into aims and objectives and then developing alternative strategies for achieving them. The process also includes the development of criteria against which the planned outcomes will eventually be evaluated. Planning can therefore be applied to a wide variety of activities which may vary in scale and which may involve short, medium or long term planning approaches.

In order to be effective, planning must utilise information which has been gathered through reviewing and forecasting the school's activities. The planning process then translates and communicates the information so that it can be used to make decisions about the way forward. Planning therefore occupies an important position as a preliminary to the budgetary design and implementation process in both locally managed and grant maintained schools.

Having established a definition of planning the following key aspects will now be examined:

- The problems of planning in education
- Different types or levels of planning
- The sequence of planning
- Criteria for effective planning

The problems of planning in education

Many people see planning as one of the hard nosed rational management tasks in organisations. However, others feel that, because of the speed of change, educational planning is very difficult and has a political rather than rational dimension. This political dimension occurs when the interests of the individuals in the organisation take priority over the organisational objectives that have been set down. There are also difficulties with the rational approach because there are, within the teaching profession and amongst the wider community, diverse views about educational aims and goals. For example, there is considerable debate about the increasing tendency to see education as a means to an end rather than as an end in itself. Once common goals have been agreed, conflict may still be generated during the rest of the planning process because people will disagree about the means of achieving those goals. All educational activities are dependent on relationships between people so there will, inevitably, be situations which give rise to disagreement as to the value of formal planning.

Despite these problems, it is our view that a proactive planning approach is appropriate to the dynamic environment in which schools find themselves, and their need to be responsive to pupils and to changing circumstances. As readers will appreciate, educational change occurs quite frequently and sometimes has to be implemented very quickly. It is much easier to respond to such change if one can switch course, yet still be working within the broad framework which has been planned. Proactive management is important because it allows for flexible responses to changing circumstances with plans and objectives in mind. This structured response is far less disruptive than reactive or crisis management which occurs if the organisation lacks a strategic sense of direction so that plans are haphazard and objectives are unclear.

It is relatively easy to plan the immediate future for oneself, but, the further away the plans must move from oneself and the present, the more difficult planning becomes. This is because of

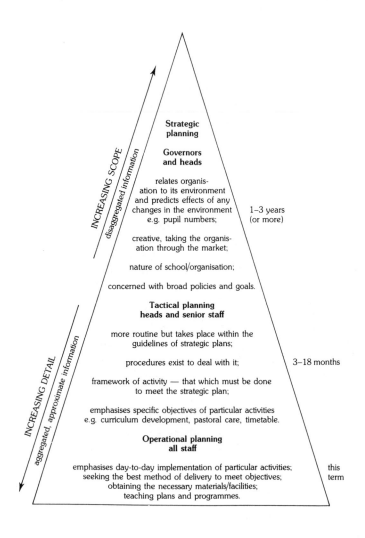

Figure 1.1 Levels of planning

the introduction of more and more unknown factors. Many teachers have felt considerable frustration when uncertainty, for example at national or local level, has been used within the school as an excuse to avoid planning beyond the immediate future. Such uncertainty only reinforces the need for flexibility in educational planning so that schools can respond rapidly to changing circumstances.

Levels of planning

A useful way to consider planning within organisations is in terms of three key levels, those of strategic, operational and tactical planning. The key features at each level can best be illustrated in Figure 1.1 from Davies et al: (1990) p.34.

The sequence of planning

The sequence of planning in a school can be seen to go through the following four stages:

Vision

This is the basic purpose and values to which the school aspires and it sets the context for the management of the school's activities. It is built on the governors' and headteacher's desires for the school over the next few years so that a framework can be set for the highest possible standards to be achieved.

Mission

The members of any organisation should have a clear idea of its purpose and this is expressed in the form of a 'mission statement' or 'corporate objective', defining the business in which the organisation is involved. This strategic activity at the level of the whole school is a planning task for the governors and head, in consultation with others, especially the staff.

Aims

The aims of the school spell out the broad path to be followed and break the mission statement down into a number of areas that can be tackled. The detail of how these are to be achieved is contained in the more focused objectives.

Objectives

Once the school aims have been stated in general terms, objectives will be set at middle management level within a school and will relate to the achievement of the aims. However, at the classroom level there may be specific objectives set for a particular session or activity. These will be drawn up by the teacher and should relate to those set by middle managers. A useful way of checking objectives is provided by an acronym which will be familiar to some readers. Objectives should be challenging and:

S	pecific
M	easurable
A	greed and Achievable
R	elevant
T	imed

Objectives will be adjusted more frequently than aims, usually at annual intervals but also more regularly if a need is shown, for example following evaluation of existing activities. It is also necessary to plan from the outset the performance indicators which should be achieved in relation to these objectives.

Criteria for effective planning

The reader may like to reflect on planning within his/her own school and to compare that experience with the following checklist (adapted from Davies et al. 1990) of factors which facilitate effective planning. Planners in school should ensure that:

1. The necessary information (external and internal) is available;
2. Clear, precise channels of communication exist in all directions;
3. Staff at all levels are committed to the project and its goals;
4. The level of planning activity is clear to those who organise meetings. It is ineffective to mix strategic issues with tactical or operational ones on an agenda because it is difficult to change focus;
5. The various sections of the school function as effective teams with clear objectives so that they know what is required of them;

6. The evaluation process is built in during the planning stage, rather than 'bolted on' afterwards.

Having established some basic concepts regarding planning, the chapter moves on to review some of the basic questions about the specific area of school development planning.

The nature and purpose of school development plans

A school development plan reviews and prioritises a school's activities in the context of national and local policies to provide a realistic strategy for efficient and effective management of the school. The plan should lead to the enhancement of the quality of education for pupils in the school. When examining the nature of school development plans, four basic areas can be considered:

1. The importance of a school development plan;
2. The internal and external uses of a school development plan;
3. Participation in the school development planning process;
4. The holistic nature of school development plans.

1.   The importance of a school development plan

All schools need to plan if they are to be efficient and effective in carrying out their educational mission. A school development plan enables the school to set attainable and observable objectives. By doing so it allows the school to assess where it is now with respect to those objectives. This provides a framework for the school to design an implementation strategy. Finally, the plan establishes structures and procedures for monitoring and evaluation over realistic timescales.

2.   The internal and external uses of a school development plan

There are a number of dimensions to the uses of the school development plan, both internally within the school and at the internal/external boundary of the school's relationships with the wider community.

The internal uses of a school development plan by the staff of a school can be seen in four key areas. Firstly the plan allows all staff to have a coherent picture of the school's activities. This is very important if they are to set their work in the overall context of the school's activities. Secondly by doing this the development plan enables staff to plan and prioritise their own work in areas such as curriculum, staffing and resources. Thirdly it provides a means of communication and coordination of aims, priorities and targets to all staff. Finally, by setting a framework it allows staff to evaluate and appraise their work.

   External uses of a school development plan can also fall into four key areas: Firstly, as a policy document that is approved by the governors it provides the basis of agreement and action by the partners in the management of the school. Secondly, because specific grants are not covered in the formula funding mechanism, the school development plan provides the basis of the school's resource bids for non-delegated categories such as capital bids or Grants for Educational Support and Training (GEST) by articulating and prioritising these within the plan. Thirdly, it provides the basis for external audit and evaluation of the school by the LEA or other external agency. As such it can provide the appraisal framework for the senior management team. Finally, as a marketing device it acts as a means of recognising and promoting the achievements of the staff, pupils and the school in general.

3. Participation in the school development planning process

When considering the role of the partners in the school and the education service in constructing and operating school development plans, the school needs to decide who is responsible for:

- Policy generation;
- Policy approval;
- Policy implementation;
- Policy administration.

   Key areas for consideration are firstly, the way in which the roles of the participants in the school development planning process can be determined and, secondly, how effective links and communications between them can be established. How do headteachers and staff develop a detailed curriculum within the broad guidelines laid down by the governors? How is this communicated to the governors so that they can have adequate information to approve the final plans? The role of the participants and the sequence of decision-making in each of these policy areas needs to be determined as a matter of priority. Equally important is the way in which policy is effectively implemented and the way that efficient administration takes place. It is necessary to determine who should take responsibility for these areas and how they are to be reported and evaluated. Roles and responsibilities are discussed in detail in Chapter Four.

4.   The holistic nature of school development plans

The school development plan should provide the mechanism for defining a school's aims and translating these into effective education. Activities can be subdivided into *core elements* which represent the main purpose of the school and *support elements* which facilitate the effective operation of the core elements. This holistic view of the school development plan is represented in Figure 1.2.

The school development plan brings all these separate activities together in one coherent document to provide a strategic picture of where the school is, where it is going; and how it intends to get there. Some people may consider that only certain major activities require planning e.g. the curriculum or future staffing. Although there will be separate, more detailed plans for each of these areas, their integration ensures that the separate plans are complementary whereas, in the past, compartmentalised planning led to overlaps and omissions. At the strategic level it is much more valuable to think of a global school development plan

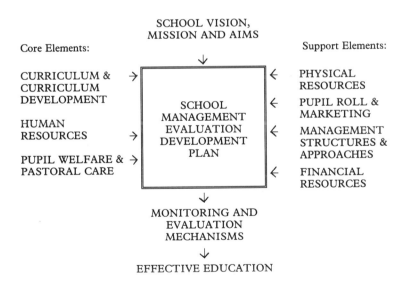

Figure 1.2   School management development plan

which brings together all core and support elements. It is not intended that this plan should be 'cast in concrete' but, rather, that it should be flexible so that the school looks ahead but remains responsive to future changes in circumstances.

Conclusion

This first chapter has set out to review the nature of planning and looks at some basic factors regarding school development planning in general. The next chapter takes a more detailed approach by examining the various stages that schools should undertake in the planning cycle.

Reference

Davies B, Ellison L, Osborne A and West-Burnham J, *Education Management for the 1990s*, Longman 1990

2 Managing the plan: the cycle of activity

The previous chapter discussed the nature and dimensions of planning in general and then explored the concept of school development plans and the reasons why they are now the central feature of the school's management activity. This chapter applies these principles of planning to the process of creating and implementing a school development plan. Early attempts to describe development planning tended to see it as an annual activity of fixed duration. This focused attention on the initial creation of plans with the schools feeling that this was the critical stage. We believe, however, that development planning should be seen as an on-going process of reviewing, forecasting, budgeting and implementing. The school development plan would summarise these activities and act as an ongoing adjustable document. The process is used to determine new developments that need to be planned and then put into operation but must also cover the majority of existing activities as these have to be maintained and managed. Thus, managing the plan involves working through a continuous cycle in order to integrate new and existing activities.

This chapter takes the reader through that cycle as shown in Figure 2.1. which should take place if the school development plan is to be effectively drawn up and implemented.

Before going any further, it is useful for governors and the senior management team to consider the way in which the development planning process is currently managed in the school. Initially, it is worth clarifying at what time in the school year the various stages in the cycle take place and what happens at each of

Figure 2.1   The school development plan cycle

the stages. It is important to identify who coordinates the activity at each of the stages and who else should be involved. In terms of communications, schools should ensure that all the partners in the process are aware of the nature of the plan and the cyclical nature of the stages. If this is not the case, an open session should be arranged at which this can be discussed. Finally, schools should ensure that the completed plan is circulated to all staff and governors and made available to parents on request.

The chapter will now provide a more detailed examination of each of the six stages of:

1. Review or audit;
2. Definition or redefinition of whole school aims;
3. Establishment of the school development plan;
4. Budgetary process;
5. Implementation of the plan; and
6. Monitoring, evaluation and reporting.

1.   Review or audit

Page 9 showed how each of the core and support elements feeds into the whole school development plan. Bearing in mind time constraints, especially in a small school, the review or audit should consider the position with regard to each of these elements. There should be a review of the current position and of anticipated trends, both within the school and within the wider context of the local community and the education service nationally. It is important that self-managing schools should consider internal reviews alongside any external reviews carried out by the LEA or by other inspectors. An internal review may use informal methods to determine the school's Strengths, Weaknesses, Opportunities and Threats (a SWOT analysis) or more formal evaluation approaches, for example the Guidelines for Review and Internal Development in Schools (GRIDS) analysis. Further information which is applicable to both primary and secondary schools concerning review by SWOT analysis can be found in *Marketing the Secondary School* (Davies and Ellison 1991). To obtain a wide range of review information it may be appropriate to consult the school's clients and potential clients such as pupils, parents, and industry. A very good example of the way in which one school carried out this process is provided at the end of the chapter. Bacup and Rawtenstall Grammar School gathered opinions from different segments of the school community on a wide range of issues.

An LEA school needs to have access to the LEA's own development plans (which are published as medium term objectives) and the curriculum policy statements and further documents related to specific groups such as the early years, post-16 education, or children with special needs. The school must also have reference material concerning national legislation and proposals.

Much of the information which is required at this review stage is already available somewhere but it needs collecting together and using to inform the debate about the way forward, either for the whole school or within one of the core or support elements. There may be the occasional need to collect new data but this process should be arranged so as not to be too onerous a task.

The chart given in Table 2.1 will act as an *aide-mémoire* when carrying out this review stage.

The management of a school may like to use the following checklist to ensure that they have not overlooked any factors. Although it is a basic list we believe that it provides a useful starting point:

- Has the school started to review each core and support element?
- How much time can be devoted to the review?

CORE ELEMENTS	SUPPORT ELEMENTS
Curriculum and curriculum development	Physical resources
	Pupil roll and marketing
Human resources	Management structures and approaches
Pupil welfare and pastoral care	Monitoring and evaluation mechanisms
	Financial resources

For each of the core and support elements:

Assess:
- Strengths
- Weaknesses
- Opportunities
- Threats

Consider:
- Changes in the local area
- Local policies and proposals
- National policies and proposals

Table 2.1   Review of the core and support elements

- Where do we find the information — governors, teaching staff, non-teaching staff, pupils (past, present and potential), parents, advisers and inspectors, the local community?
- Who collects the information?
- Who summarises the information?
- How are the governors involved?

2.   Definition or redefinition of the whole school aims

As was shown in Chapter One, the four stages of developing vision, mission, aims and objectives provide the sequence that each school needs to follow in order to determine the direction that it will take. The partners in the school must share a common vision of that school and work together to realise the vision through its many activities. It is important to discuss the nature of this vision and, depending on the outcomes of the review/audit process, to adjust the vision in order to provide the product and service which is both wanted and needed in the existing and future educational environment. The building and sharing of this vision will take time and may involve meetings of various different groups, for example governors with staff (including non-teaching staff).

Once the vision has been shared, the mission statement for the whole school will be created or adjusted so that it is brought into focus. All partners will then have a clear view and understanding of the school's goals, values and its aspirations for the pupils in its care. With the mission statement in mind, the aims of the school are then considered and defined or redefined, as necessary.

Both the mission statement and the whole school aims which are developed from it 'belong' to the organisation. Aims set out the broad path to be followed by the school as it attempts to meet the wants and needs of the clients. An aim is created by taking a key word from the mission statement and turning it into statements of intent (see page 17). The school can then focus on these statements when deciding the objectives and activities which are needed in order to realise the vision and the mission of the school.

There must be a sense of ownership of the aims in order to increase the chance of their being achieved. Each school should, therefore, decide how best to review and redefine its aims. In many cases the teaching staff already participate fully in this activity but the governors and senior management might consider broadening the process to include non-teaching staff and the parents who, after all, are a very significant client group. While there are problems of obtaining agreement between the partners it is important to discuss, to have a common view, and to reach a consensus.

Vision, mission and aims are broad-based so that frequent, major changes are unlikely but the need to redefine them will be largely determined by the rate of change in the educational environment.

The school must now address itself to determining what needs to be done in order to achieve the aims. Where previously we have been considering the broad concepts of vision and purpose, when it comes to objectives the emphasis shifts to measurable activities. Once the school aims have been stated in general terms, corporate or whole school objectives will be developed and will relate to the achievement of these aims (and thus to the mission statement). Objectives are often set in a short to medium term context (up to three years) as a tactical or operational planning device. They are a way of specifying what must be done across the areas of the school within a given time and, as such, will need to be redefined more frequently than aims, usually at annual intervals.

The whole school objectives will:

- Provide a coherent approach across the different areas of the school;
- Define narrower targets in order to achieve the school's mission and aims;
- Quantify those targets which the school can realistically achieve.

If they are understood by all staff, whole school objectives will form a framework on which the operation of the school can be based. If purposeful, goal directed activity is to take place, the setting of specific objectives will be necessary for all elements within the school such as for the curriculum, pastoral care, human resources and marketing. Page 6 outlined the various management points to bear in mind when planning objectives. Most significantly, objectives should be quantifiable and expressed in concrete terms. It is important that these specific objectives are set in relation to the strategic perspective identified in the long term planning process.

An example of the process

The following sequence of activities was introduced in the previous chapter:

It involves a process of developing shared visions into activities so that the school's product and service match the clients' wants and needs. A practical example of this definition process is demonstrated in Figure 2.2 from Davies and Ellison (1991). There is a broad vision for the school and from this a mission statement has been developed. One aspect of the mission statement (challenging environment) is taken and aims are developed. Finally, one of the aims (to provide stimulating and challenging teaching materials) is translated into objectives through which it can be realised.

By going through this process, clear objectives can be developed which relate to the achievement of the school's mission and aims. These objectives will be used to guide the activities required and to measure performance at a later stage. If all the partners have a clear view of what needs doing and if this relates to client wants and needs, then the school will demonstrate quality in its management thinking and in its educational outcomes. Readers may wish to use the following checklist to

VISION   of a caring school which is outward looking
                        and intellectually stretches children of all
                        abilities.

MISSION   *Brentwich School fosters academic and
                        personal development in a caring and
                        challenging environment so that each
                        individual can achieve his or her full potential.*

AIMS   1.   *To provide stimulating and challenging
                        teaching materials.*

                  2.   To provide extension and support materials for
                        different ability levels.

                  3.   To develop high expectation levels of individual
                        performance.

                  4.   To set targets for each group and individual.

OBJECTIVES   1.   To investigate the type of materials which fulfil
                        Aim 1 above.

                  2.   To provide time and support for staff to
                        examine approaches and materials available
                        and to adapt them if necessary.

                  3.   To evaluate the use of such materials in
                        increasing pupil involvement and learning.

Figure 2.2   Translating the vision into practice

review their positions in relation to this stage of the cycle:

- Is there a shared vision of what the school is trying to achieve?
- Is there a mission statement which articulates that vision? Does this statement need revising?
- Does the school have a statement of aims?
- When was this statement last re-examined and rewritten if necessary?
- Is the whole school staff (teaching and non-teaching) involved in defining/redefining the aims (which reflect the purpose of the *whole* school)?
- How are governors involved in the process?
- How are parents involved in the process?
- Are the aims realistic within the context of the school? Can they be achieved?
- Are the aims concise?
- How are the aims communicated to staff, governors and parents?
- Are the aims well known to staff, governors and parents?

3. Establishment of the school development plan

When the earlier stages in the cycle have been carried out the school will be in a position to establish its development plan. This will be achieved by translating the general aims into action through laying down specific objectives and making overall plans on a three year basis, with more detailed plans on a one year basis. This overview at the whole school level will draw on the detailed individual plans from each of the core and support elements which are shown in Table 2.1 on page 14.

Guidance on creating the separate plans for each element is given in Chapter Three. For each of these elements staff (and perhaps governors) will have worked through the planning process by generating alternatives, prioritising both in the long and the short term and, later, choosing between alternatives in the decision-making process.

At the whole school level, the governors and senior management will be presented with alternative courses of action (with costs) and they will then apply criteria in order to make final decisions. Plans may have to be readjusted, especially if there are resource constraints, hence the feedback loop (*see* page 12) between this stage and the next stage, that of going through the budgetary process.

The outline activity plans will then be presented for the whole school and for each element. When creating the school development plan document, the partners may find the following format as in Table 2.2 useful for the presentation of information:

Section One: A profile of the school, including its aims

Section Two: A summary of trends (internal and external)

Section Three: A central plan giving medium term developments

Section Four: An action plan for the coming year to include:

  ● short term objectives

  ● targets, tasks, timing and indicators of success

  ● resource implications

Table 2.2:   Components of a whole school development plan

The action plan will give an overall picture of the proposed activities for the school. It will be created by integrating information from the separate plans for each of the core and support areas. Further detail about the presentation of the plan is given in Chapters Five, Seven and Nine.

The school may wish to reflect on its present school development plan by considering the following checklist questions:

  ● Does the school have plans for each of the core and support elements?
  ● Has the Governing Body received a summary of the priorities in each area?
  ● Who puts all the information together to produce the whole school plan?
  ● What is the timescale of this activity?
  ● How does the plan link with the budgetary process and the financial year?

4. The budgetary process

As with the overall school development plan, the budgetary

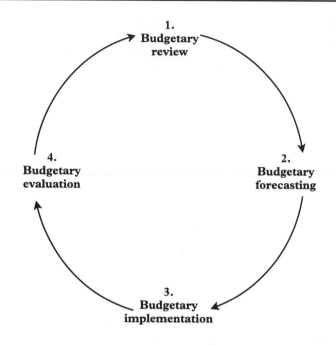

Figure 2.3 The budgetary cycle

process is a continuous cycle of activity. It sets the *educational priorities* into a *financial context* and can be seen to comprise four key stages as in Figure 2.3.

The following is intended as general advice to provide useful reference points for schools undertaking the budgetary process within the overall school development planning process. Before the budgetary process starts, it is necessary to clarify the principles and procedures which will be followed in a particular school. The main issue which needs to be considered is the extent to which the partners in the educational process are involved in the budgetary process. The roles and responsibilities of these partners (governors, staff and parents) need to be clear from the outset. The extent to which they are to be consulted or to take part in the decision-making process needs to be fully understood by those who may feel involved. Particular problems arise if people think that they are being asked to make decisions in this area when they are, in fact, only being canvassed for their opinions.

1. Budgetary review

Data which will inform this review are being gathered all year round because the school will be constantly monitoring its income and expenditure pattern. However, the budgetary review which is carried out on an annual basis is much more than this. It is the opportunity to stand back and assess the financial implications of current activities. Is the school balancing its income and expenditure? Are there significant levels of over or underspending in particular areas? Are there current opportunities that will allow the school to reallocate expenditure and enhance learning outputs for the pupils?

It is important, therefore, to review income and expenditure patterns in all the core and support elements in order to gain information on current performance and also data for changes in the next budgetary round. This should provide early warning of the financial effects of change and of the provision necessary to accommodate continuing trends or shifting patterns in these elements. Schools should be able to make increasing use of computer-based systems such as the Schools Information and Management System (SIMS) as a management and review tool rather than as a mere administrative tool. Thus, 'What if?' questions can be asked assuming different scenarios of current policy options or shifts in them. Having established a clear picture of the current budgetary position and of the possible outcomes of maintaining or altering policies, the school then needs to move on to the next stage of the budgetary cycle.

2.   Budgetary forecasting

It is a serious mistake to view budgetary decisions within a one year time frame. A large number of decisions have financial implications that spread over a number of years. Deciding to use one particular learning scheme rather than another can have a considerable impact on costs in terms of the resources that have to be renewed in future years. Similarly, choosing between two staff appointments may result in a salary saving of £6,000 in the first year and, even though the 'cheaper' member of staff moves up the incremental salary scale, the savings over a five year period can be in excess of £20,000. While it is important for a school to aim for a balanced budget, over or underspending has to be set in the context of the level of future income. A marginal overspend is not so serious in a school which is increasing its pupil roll, and hence its income, as it would be in a school with a falling roll and income.

The school needs to engage in a budgetary forecasting exercise that predicts income and expenditure over a three year period to be able to set its immediate decisions in context. Thus, the school must forecast the pupil roll over three years and translate this (by using the formula funding mechanism) into an income forecast for the three years. Similarly, non-formula sources of income will need the same assessment and prediction. On the expenditure side, the continuation of current expenditure policies and patterns will have to be costed together with any proposed expenditure changes coming from the reviews of the core and support elements. When this has been done the governors will have a clearer context in which to make their annual budgetary decisions.

3. Budgetary implementation

The important stage of implementing the budget needs to be started well before the beginning of the financial year. It is at this stage that final decisions are made about which proposed activities can be resourced and which must be postponed or rejected. Many expenditure items represent fixed costs so that administrators can, first of all, use the previous year as a framework in order to 'pencil' in standard continuing items. Adjustments can be made to allow for policy changes which have been approved. The school would need to take account of the existing review and forecasting exercise and then work through the detailed headings of income and expenditure step by step. Up to this point, decisions would probably be made by a subgroup but when completed, the final budget will need formal approval at a full governors' meeting.

4. Budgetary evaluation

This stage, which is often neglected or reduced to an examination of the outturn figures, could be carried out by a subgroup. We suggest that the process should be carried out in the summer term when outturn figures are available and when staff and others will be in a position to make early comments on the effectiveness of expenditure over the previous financial year. This may be the group which will be planning the budget for the following April. When evaluating the budgetary process, consideration should be given not only to the financial outturn and any adjustments that have to be made but also to the way in which the budget has been managed.

Managers in schools may wish to consider the following questions when planning or evaluating their approach to the budgetary process:

- Who is involved in the budgetary process?
- What are the roles and responsibilities of governors, staff

and parents? To what extent are they consulted or take part
in the decision-making process?

- How is the review to be structured?
- Is the resourcing of certain areas to be examined in more
  depth on an occasional basis?
- Who is to summarise the review information, indicating
  priorities?
- When is the summary to be presented to the Governing
  Body?
- Who is involved with making forecasts?
- Who provides the data?
- Who makes final decisions about choices and allocations?
- Are these decisions based on the priorities identified in the
  school development plan?
- What is the nature of the evaluation of spending decisions?
- What is the nature of the evaluation of the process of
  making decisions about expenditure?

5. Implementation of the plan

Once the school development plan has been approved and
resourced, the one year detailed plan will be implemented. In areas
where change is being introduced, schools will have to consider the
way in which the change process is to be managed as well as the
nature of the change. It is worth reflecting on the well known
maxim that 'the way that you manage a change can be as important
as the change that you manage'. It is not sufficient to have a first
rate development plan if lack of commitment by staff or lack of
communication of information to them makes it impossible to
implement that plan effectively. If school managers have considered very carefully how the plan is drawn up, allowing for
appropriate participation, then at the implementation stage there
will be similar levels of ownership and commitment by the staff
who must implement the plan. Before and during the implementation stage governors and the senior management team should:

- Circulate the development plan;
- Explain the need for change;
- Phase the introduction of changes;
- Designate responsibility for overseeing the change process;
- Make available the resources to implement the change;
- Allow adequate preparation time;
- Allow opportunities to share concerns;
- Allocate time and other resources for staff development;
- Clarify the way in which success will be evaluated;
- Support staff during the change; and
- Communicate clearly at all times.

6. Monitoring, evaluation and reporting

Monitoring of the aims and objectives in action is a constant and consistent activity. There also needs to be some form of *evaluation* in order to assess whether the plans, once implemented, have effectively achieved the objectives set. Evaluation, therefore, looks at outcomes and uses evidence from monitoring. The nature of the monitoring and evaluation should be determined at the planning stage and it is therefore considered in Chapter Three as one of the support elements which contributes to the whole school development plan.

In reflecting on its monitoring and evaluation process the school should consider the following checklist:

- Who monitors the school in action?
- How is the monitoring carried out?
- How are the governors kept informed on a termly basis?
- Who evaluates the school's activities?
- How is evaluation carried out?
- How are the results of the evaluation used?
- How are the parents kept informed?
- Who prepares the annual report for parents?
- Who prepares the annual report for the LEA (where appropriate)?
- Who prepares the financial report?

Having worked through the cycle of management activity, the information from the evaluation stage can be used to inform the next review or audit as the cycle continues again. Vision, mission, and aims will be checked for their continued relevance and the various components of the school development plan will be adjusted as necessary.

Conclusion

This chapter has set the context for the school development plan by establishing a cycle of activity which each school should follow in managing its planning process. The detail that should be considered in each of the core and support elements of the school development plan will now be outlined in Chapter Three.

Reference

Davies B and Ellison L, *Marketing the Secondary School*, Longman 1991

Figure 2.4   School exemplar

BRGS SCHOOL DEVELOPMENT PLAN (SDP) AUDIT STAGE

Introduction

The purpose of the SDP is to aid the development of areas of the school's organisation and practices so that we can improve further the education of our young people. The construction of an SDP is a requirement of the government. The SDP will be the main factor influencing where we spend money and where we concentrate particular efforts over the next five years; it is, therefore, a very important process.

The process of producing the SDP has the following stages:

Stage 1: The audit   The school reviews its strengths and weaknesses and then identifies which areas need to be developed. (Spring term 1991)

Stage 2: Plan construction   The priorities for development in the next five years are identified. Detailed action plans, with targets, tasks and criteria for measuring success are constructed for the first year of the plan and roles and responsibilities are assigned. (Summer term 1991)

Stage 3: Implementation of the SDP   The first year of the plan will be put into practice from September 1991.

Stage 4: Evaluation of the SDP   The plan will be monitored and updated each year so that it always extends for five years.

What to do

The purpose of this document is to carry out the audit stage.

You are asked to:

1. Think about the strengths and weaknesses of the school. Checklists are given to guide your thinking.
2. Decide which areas should be developed.
3. Suggest when these developments should be implemented.

Exact details of what to do in each of these three steps now follow:

1. *Strengths and weaknesses*   This document includes checklists for all aspects of the school so that you can comment on as many as you wish. As this is a large amount of work, it is felt that you should think particularly about the following areas:
    I. *Policy/heads of department group* — whole-school matters relating to all aspects of school viz:
        ● Philosophy;
        ● Management;
        ● Curriculum;
        ● Staff;
        ● Resources; and
        ● Constituency.
    II. *Heads of year meeting* — whole-school issues and the pastoral area relating to:
        ● Philosophy;
        ● Management;
        ● Curriculum especially care and guidance; and
        ● Constituency.
    III. *Governors* — whole-school areas relating to:
        ● Philosophy;
        ● Curriculum — especially external links;
        ● Resources; and

B

- Staff — especially management,
  appointments,
  legal responsibilities; and
- Constituency.
  IV. *Departmental meetings* — topics within the department relating to:
  - Management;
  - Curriculum, excluding care and guidance;
  - Resources; and
  - Staff.
  V. *Year tutor meetings* — topics within the year relating to:
  - Curriculum — care and guidance.
  VI. *Caretaker and cleaners* — topics relating to:
  - Management;
  - Resources; and
  - Staff.
  VII. *Secretaries and resource technician* — topics relating to:
  - Management;
  - Resources; and
  - Staff.
  VIII. *Individual teaching staff* — topics relating to:
  - Philosophy;
  - Management; and
  - Staff.

As you work through the checklists you might feel that some items do no apply to your area: if so miss them out.

You should return the document to Dr. Robinson after you have finished your discussions. You might wish to keep a copy for yourself.

As you discuss each item in the checklist, tick the appropriate column to show:

- Strength — something we do well;
- Satisfactory;
- Weakness — something we are doing badly and could be improved; or
- Omission — something we are not doing at all that we should be doing.

2. *Areas to be developed* — When you have finished each section, decide which areas (if any) should be developed. They might be current weaknesses or omissions, or areas which are already satisfactory or are strengths and need further development to meet future demands. Write short statements to describe them on the sheet headed *Areas for Development* which is at the end of this document. Examples from the geography department might be:
3.2(d) New scheme of work for National Curriculum for   Year 1
and for Year 2
and for Year 3

3. *Timetable for developments* — when you have finished discussing checklists, return to the sheet *Areas for Development* and write the year in which you feel the development should be implemented. The geography department examples would be:
3.2(d) New scheme of work for National Curriculum for Year 1 91–92
and for Year 2 92–93
and for Year 3 93–94

Please remember that we have to plan in outline for the next five years. Research has shown that the plan should be realistic, neither too ambitious nor insufficiently demanding. There should be no more than three or four major priorities in each year in each department. Each major priority may contain a number of elements.

Checklists for the auditing of BRGS

Meeting(s) of ....

or

Individual's name ....

1 Philosophy and ethos checklist

Written statements of the following should already exist. Together they indicate the philosophy and ethos of the school. To what extent do you feel you are aware of the school's aims and procedures in these areas?

	STRENGTH	SATISFACTORY	WEAKNESS	OMISSION
a. Statement of general aims	☐	☐	☐	☐
b. School Development Plan, incorporating National Curriculum requirements and other curriculum initiatives	☐	☐	☐	☐
c. Records of Achievement and arrangements for reporting on pupils' progress	☐	☐	☐	☐
d. Organisation of teaching groups	☐	☐	☐	☐
e. Children with special needs	☐	☐	☐	☐
f. RE and collective worship	☐	☐	☐	☐
g. Arrangements for entering pupils for public examinations	☐	☐	☐	☐
h. Careers education	☐	☐	☐	☐
i. Links with industry	☐	☐	☐	☐
j. Homework requirements	☐	☐	☐	☐
k. Pastoral care	☐	☐	☐	☐
l. Personal and social education	☐	☐	☐	☐
m. Health education	☐	☐	☐	☐
n. Sex education	☐	☐	☐	☐
o. School discipline	☐	☐	☐	☐
p. School uniform in years 1 to 5 and the code of dress in the sixth form	☐	☐	☐	☐
q. Equal opportunities	☐	☐	☐	☐
r. Education within a multicultural society	☐	☐	☐	☐
s. Transition arrangements from primary and other feeder schools to BRGS and from BRGS to other establishments	☐	☐	☐	☐
t. Staff development	☐	☐	☐	☐
u. Links with external agencies	☐	☐	☐	☐
v. Admissions policy	☐	☐	☐	☐
w. Charging policy	☐	☐	☐	☐

2. Management checklist

		STRENGTH	SATISFACTORY	WEAKNESS	OMISSION
a.	Management structure to audit, prioritise, construct, implement, monitor and evaluate the SDP (School Development Plan)	☐	☐	☐	☐
b.	General management structure	☐	☐	☐	☐
c.	● Terms of reference	☐	☐	☐	☐
	● Decision-making procedures	☐	☐	☐	☐
d.	● Communication of minutes and decisions	☐	☐	☐	☐
	Consultation with/involvement of/communication with:				
e.	● headteacher	☐	☐	☐	☐
f.	● teachers	☐	☐	☐	☐
g.	● non-teaching staff	☐	☐	☐	☐
h.	● governors	☐	☐	☐	☐
i.	● parents	☐	☐	☐	☐
j.	● other professionals outside the school	☐	☐	☐	☐
k.	● pupils	☐	☐	☐	☐
l.	Identification of staff development needs in terms of school needs and in terms of individual career development	☐	☐	☐	☐
m.	Delegation and areas of responsibility	☐	☐	☐	☐
n.	Monitoring and evaluation	☐	☐	☐	☐

3. Curriculum checklist

	STRENGTH	SATISFACTORY	WEAKNESS	OMISSION

3.1 Pupil learning and teaching

3.1.1 Pupil learning

	STRENGTH	SATISFACTORY	WEAKNESS	OMISSION
a. Pupils are able to work collaboratively and independently	☐	☐	☐	☐
b. Pupils are encouraged to develop initiative	☐	☐	☐	☐
c. Concentration and attentiveness of pupils	☐	☐	☐	☐
d. Pupil involvement and appropriate behaviour throughout the school	☐	☐	☐	☐
e. Pupils are able to meet learning demands	☐	☐	☐	☐
f. Pupils are aware of the strengths and weaknesses of their own performance	☐	☐	☐	☐
g. Pupils have the opportunities and skills to extend their learning and to define learning tasks	☐	☐	☐	☐
h. There is progression and continuity in learning	☐	☐	☐	☐
i. Individual learning needs are being met i.e. match and challenge	☐	☐	☐	☐
j. Pupils receive a wide and balanced range of learning experiences	☐	☐	☐	☐
k. The work observed meets required statements of attainment at an appropriate level	☐	☐	☐	☐
l. Home and community involvement in learning	☐	☐	☐	☐

3.1.2 Teaching

	STRENGTH	SATISFACTORY	WEAKNESS	OMISSION
a. Social, cultural and linguistic backgrounds are recognised and valued in the learning process. Pupils experience a balanced curriculum in accordance with the principle of entitlement as expressed in the:	☐	☐	☐	☐
b. School's curriculum policy;	☐	☐	☐	☐
c. Requirements of the National Curriculum;	☐	☐	☐	☐
Work:	☐	☐	☐	☐
d. Is planned;	☐	☐	☐	☐
e. Builds on and reinforces existing learning;	☐	☐	☐	☐
f. Meets the learning needs of pupils; and	☐	☐	☐	☐
g. Uses suitable resources.	☐	☐	☐	☐
h. High expectations of pupil performance	☐	☐	☐	☐
i. Repertoire of professional skills suitable for the particular curriculum area/subject and the context in which learning takes place	☐	☐	☐	☐

	STRENGTH	SATISFACTORY	WEAKNESS	OMISSION
j. Links within and across subjects and curriculum areas	☐	☐	☐	☐
k. Teacher has sufficient knowledge of subject and methodology	☐	☐	☐	☐
l. Ordered learning environment which allows curriculum goals to be realised	☐	☐	☐	☐
m. Pupils are given opportunities to develop and practise the skills of independent and collaborative learning	☐	☐	☐	☐
n. Teacher–pupil and pupil–pupil relationships are sensitive and sufficiently ordered to allow productive work to take place	☐	☐	☐	☐
o. Teachers take account of follow-up, continuity and reinforcement in the learning process	☐	☐	☐	☐
p. Agreed scheme for the monitoring, assessment and recording of pupils' work	☐	☐	☐	☐

3.2 Schemes of work

	STRENGTH	SATISFACTORY	WEAKNESS	OMISSION
a. Cross-curricular school policies for example on special needs, equal opportunities, economic awareness, world of work, homework, multiculturalism, careers education and guidance, health education	☐	☐	☐	☐
b. Subject-specific policies where appropriate	☐	☐	☐	☐
c. Relationship with the school's aims and philosophy	☐	☐	☐	☐
d. Agreement with National Curriculum/Governors' policy requirements and other current initiatives	☐	☐	☐	☐
e. Continuity, progression and differentiation in schemes of work	☐	☐	☐	☐
f. Expression of purposes and learning objectives	☐	☐	☐	☐
g. Variety of methods and approaches	☐	☐	☐	☐
h. Relevant content	☐	☐	☐	☐
i. Appropriate resources	☐	☐	☐	☐
j. Attention to learning outcomes	☐	☐	☐	☐
k. Assessment/evaluation policies	☐	☐	☐	☐
l. Recording and reporting	☐	☐	☐	☐
m. Procedures for review	☐	☐	☐	☐
n. Accessibility of documentation for staff, governors, parents	☐	☐	☐	☐
o. Appreciation by staff of the particular contribution of a subject or aspect to the whole curriculum	☐	☐	☐	☐
p. Appropriate classroom application	☐	☐	☐	☐
q. Resource compatibility	☐	☐	☐	☐

	STRENGTH	SATISFACTORY	WEAKNESS	OMISSION

3.3 Assessment

3.3.1 Use of assessment instruments

a. Appropriate completion and use of internal records eg. transfer documents, pupil records, exam/test results, records of achievement, reports to parents, parental consultations, parents' evenings — ☐ ☐ ☐ ☐

b. Appropriate completion and use of external records eg. specific individual assessments including those of special needs, GCSE, other instruments — ☐ ☐ ☐ ☐

c. Suitable use of standardised assessments eg. NFER and other tests — ☐ ☐ ☐ ☐

d. Suitable use of statutory assessments i.e. those associated with National Curriculum, 1981 Act procedure etc. — ☐ ☐ ☐ ☐

e. Effective record keeping using previous records and information and of classroom, departmental and whole school systems — ☐ ☐ ☐ ☐

3.3.2 Management of assessment

a. School and departmental policy statements consistent with school aims and philosophy — ☐ ☐ ☐ ☐

- Effective implementation through: — ☐ ☐ ☐ ☐

b. Clear delegation of responsibility — ☐ ☐ ☐ ☐

c. Manageable reporting systems — ☐ ☐ ☐ ☐

d. Appropriate use of diagnostic, formative and summative assessment — ☐ ☐ ☐ ☐

e. Strategies for continuity and review — ☐ ☐ ☐ ☐

f. Communication pertinent to staff, parents, governors, media — ☐ ☐ ☐ ☐

g. Reports to parents — ☐ ☐ ☐ ☐

h. Parents' evenings — ☐ ☐ ☐ ☐

i. Parental consultations/interviews — ☐ ☐ ☐ ☐

j. Fulfilment of statutory information requirements — ☐ ☐ ☐ ☐

k. Range of assessment techniques, eg. observation, dialogue, listening, questioning, tests, tasks, pupil self-assessment — ☐ ☐ ☐ ☐

l. Teacher's knowledge of individual pupil's ability and progress — ☐ ☐ ☐ ☐

Marking:

m. Supports learning — ☐ ☐ ☐ ☐

n. Regular and up-to-date — ☐ ☐ ☐ ☐

	STRENGTH	SATISFACTORY	WEAKNESS	OMISSION
o. Stresses positive achievement	☐	☐	☐	☐
p. Matches curriculum objectives	☐	☐	☐	☐
q. Actively involves pupils, where appropriate	☐	☐	☐	☐
r. Conforms to an agreed school or departmental policy	☐	☐	☐	☐

3.4 Organisation and management of the curriculum
3.4.1 Planning

	STRENGTH	SATISFACTORY	WEAKNESS	OMISSION
a. Pattern of meetings to meet the curriculum and organisational aims of the school	☐	☐	☐	☐
• Decision-making involving:				
b. Staff	☐	☐	☐	☐
c. Short and long-term planning	☐	☐	☐	☐
d. Recording of decisions taken	☐	☐	☐	☐
e. Implementation of decisions taken	☐	☐	☐	☐
f. Effective internal and external communication	☐	☐	☐	☐
g. Realistic job descriptions	☐	☐	☐	☐
h. Long and short-term planning at all levels	☐	☐	☐	☐

3.4.2 Pupil time

	STRENGTH	SATISFACTORY	WEAKNESS	OMISSION
a. Reasonable amount of time is allocated for all pupils to meet the obligations of the National Curriculum	☐	☐	☐	☐
b. Consultation with the head of department or coordinator in this allocation	☐	☐	☐	☐

3.4.3 Space and facilities

	STRENGTH	SATISFACTORY	WEAKNESS	OMISSION
a. Facilities and accommodation meet the school's curriculum aims and the objectives of the National Curriculum	☐	☐	☐	☐
b. Consultation with the head of department or coordinator in this allocation	☐	☐	☐	☐
c. Cost-effective use of space and facilities	☐	☐	☐	☐
d. Delegation of responsibility for the general oversight of space and facilities	☐	☐	☐	☐
e. Optimum use of specialist and non-specialist accommodation	☐	☐	☐	☐
f. Review of the provision	☐	☐	☐	☐

3.4.4 Material resources

	STRENGTH	SATISFACTORY	WEAKNESS	OMISSION
a. Essential resources are available to meet the school's curriculum aims	☐	☐	☐	☐
b. Whole-school system of allocation, known and understood by staff	☐	☐	☐	☐

	STRENGTH	SATISFACTORY	WEAKNESS	OMISSION
● Head of department or co-ordinator:				
c. Identified needs and costs	☐	☐	☐	☐
d. Recorded and spent allocation accordingly	☐	☐	☐	☐
e. Makes resources available and sees that they are used effectively	☐	☐	☐	☐
f. Monitors and evaluates the use and care of those resources	☐	☐	☐	☐

3.4.5 Grouping
● Pupil groupings in size and composition:

	STRENGTH	SATISFACTORY	WEAKNESS	OMISSION
a. Reflect the aims and objectives of the school	☐	☐	☐	☐
b. Reflect the curricular needs in the subject or aspect area for all pupils (eg. those with special needs)	☐	☐	☐	☐
c. Enhance the teaching and learning	☐	☐	☐	☐
d. Economically viable	☐	☐	☐	☐
e. Arrangements are reviewed regularly	☐	☐	☐	☐
f. Constraints affecting pupil groupings are understood by staff	☐	☐	☐	☐

3.5 Care and guidance
3.5.1 Philosophy

	STRENGTH	SATISFACTORY	WEAKNESS	OMISSION
a. School includes a statement on care and guidance within its overall aims	☐	☐	☐	☐
b. Recognition of the importance of care and guidance throughout the curriculum	☐	☐	☐	☐
c. Programme for care and guidance is informed by an awareness of the rights and requirements of individuals and groups in a pluralist society	☐	☐	☐	☐

3.5.2 Organisation

	STRENGTH	SATISFACTORY	WEAKNESS	OMISSION
a. Policy for implementing the school's philosophy	☐	☐	☐	☐
b. Effective operation of this policy by staff and pupils	☐	☐	☐	☐

3.5.3 Recording and records of achievement

	STRENGTH	SATISFACTORY	WEAKNESS	OMISSION
a. Developed instruments for collecting recording, retrieving and disseminating information including that relating to extra curricular and extra-mural activities	☐	☐	☐	☐
b. Pupils are positively involved in the processes	☐	☐	☐	☐

3.5.4 External links

	STRENGTH	SATISFACTORY	WEAKNESS	OMISSION
a. Links are developed with the home and community including industry and commerce	☐	☐	☐	☐

	STRENGTH	SATISFACTORY	WEAKNESS	OMISSION
b. Support services are used effectively	☐	☐	☐	☐
c. Effective links with other phases of education	☐	☐	☐	☐

3.5.5 Transition
a. Systematic approach for identifying and supporting pupils' needs at transition points, including post-school

☐	☐	☐	☐

3.5.6 Cross-curricular issues and themes

	STRENGTH	SATISFACTORY	WEAKNESS	OMISSION
a. Appropriately resourced programme for personal and social education	☐	☐	☐	☐
b. Agreed programme of sex education	☐	☐	☐	☐
c. Health education programme	☐	☐	☐	☐
d. Careers education and guidance programme	☐	☐	☐	☐
e. Coverage of gender and multicultural issues	☐	☐	☐	☐
f. Attention to the special needs of pupils	☐	☐	☐	☐

3.5.7 Discipline
a. Effective policy for discipline with procedures for rewards and sanctions

☐	☐	☐	☐

b. Procedures conform with the Governors' statement on discipline where they have chosen to produce such a statement

☐	☐	☐	☐

3.5.8 Attendance and punctuality
a. Policy which encourages high levels of attendance and punctuality

☐	☐	☐	☐

4. Resources checklist

	STRENGTH	SATISFACTORY	WEAKNESS	OMISSION

4.1 Resource provision
4.1.1 Site

	STRENGTH	SATISFACTORY	WEAKNESS	OMISSION
a. Provides a safe environment	☐	☐	☐	☐
b. Site and its layout meet the curriculum and organisational needs of the school	☐	☐	☐	☐

4.1.2 Buildings

a. Provide a clean, healthy environment	☐	☐	☐	☐
b. Meet the curriculum and organisational needs of the school	☐	☐	☐	☐

4.1.3 Furniture and fittings

a. Furniture and fittings are of the suitable type, size and quantity to facilitate curriculum provision	☐	☐	☐	☐

4.1.4 Books equipment and other materials

a. Sufficient books, equipment and other resources to facilitate effective learning	☐	☐	☐	☐

4.1.5 Staff: teaching and non-teaching

a. School has recruited and deployed staff to meet and support the National Curriculum requirements and Governors' recommendations	☐	☐	☐	☐
b. School policy for the use of relief staff	☐	☐	☐	☐

4.1.6 Support

a. Resources for effective administration	☐	☐	☐	☐

4.1.7 Health and safety

a. Health and safety requirements have been considered as part of the development of resources	☐	☐	☐	☐

4.2 Budgetary Decisions

a. School policy to determine the allocation of the budget	☐	☐	☐	☐
b. Mechanism for making budgetary decisions	☐	☐	☐	☐
c. Documentation to support the budgetary process	☐	☐	☐	☐
d. Monitoring of the budgetary process and planned periodic review	☐	☐	☐	☐

5. Staff: teaching and non-teaching checklist

	STRENGTH	SATISFACTORY	WEAKNESS	OMISSION

5.1 Management

a. Effective communication policies and practices with staff ☐ ☐ ☐ ☐

b. Effective policies and practices of delegation and accountability ☐ ☐ ☐ ☐

c. Effective leadership ☐ ☐ ☐ ☐

d. Effective negotiation about the deployment of support service staff ☐ ☐ ☐ ☐

5.2 Appointment

• Documentation concerning selection is:

a. Consistent with the school policy ☐ ☐ ☐ ☐

b. Consistent with the school's budget and requirements of the National Curriculum ☐ ☐ ☐ ☐

c. Conforming to legal requirements ☐ ☐ ☐ ☐

d. Covering the total selection process ☐ ☐ ☐ ☐

e. Available to applicants ☐ ☐ ☐ ☐

f. Subject to evaluation ☐ ☐ ☐ ☐

• Selection procedures are:

g. Consistent with school policy ☐ ☐ ☐ ☐

h. Conforming to legal requirements ☐ ☐ ☐ ☐

i. Subject to evaluation ☐ ☐ ☐ ☐

5.3 Induction

a. School policy exists ☐ ☐ ☐ ☐

b. Support and development during the first year of appointment to the school ☐ ☐ ☐ ☐

c. Planned support for supply staff ☐ ☐ ☐ ☐

5.4 Deployment

• Effective deployment within the terms of conditions of service including:

a. Match of qualifications and experience to responsibilities ☐ ☐ ☐ ☐

b. Equity of teaching load including non-contact time ☐ ☐ ☐ ☐

c. Evaluation of deployment procedures ☐ ☐ ☐ ☐

	STRENGTH	SATISFACTORY	WEAKNESS	OMISSION

5.5 Development
a. Existence of staff development and appraisal pro-
    gramme which is integrated within a whole school
    development plan   ☐ ☐ ☐ ☐
b. Involvement of staff in the formulation of the pro-
    gramme   ☐ ☐ ☐ ☐
c. Effective operation of a programme which incorporates
    short, medium and long term goals   ☐ ☐ ☐ ☐

5.6 Legal responsibilities
a. School policy which has been agreed by the governing
    body in the light of Employment Legislation,
    Industrial Relations, Equal Opportunities, Remunera-
    tion of Teachers   ☐ ☐ ☐ ☐
b. Awareness and understanding of the relevant codes of
    practice on discharging such responsibilities   ☐ ☐ ☐ ☐

6. Constituency (governors, parents and community) checklist

	STRENGTH	SATISFACTORY	WEAKNESS	OMISSION

6.1 Aims and Policies

a. School includes within its aims a statement on relationships with other agencies and the community ☐ ☐ ☐ ☐

b. Statement takes account of the role of the local community as expressed in legislation and guidelines, for example governing bodies, parents, local industry, voluntary bodies and the police ☐ ☐ ☐ ☐

c. Teaching and non-teaching staff are aware of these aims and policies ☐ ☐ ☐ ☐

d. School has a programme to review, develop and promote its reputation within the community ☐ ☐ ☐ ☐

6.2 Implementation

a. Effective communication ☐ ☐ ☐ ☐

b. Mutually beneficial relationships with the community ☐ ☐ ☐ ☐

c. Involvement in the school by the community ☐ ☐ ☐ ☐

d. Involvement of parents in the life and work of the school ☐ ☐ ☐ ☐

e. Use of resources and premises by members of the community ☐ ☐ ☐ ☐

6.3 Review

a. Evidence of processes of evaluation and any action taken ☐ ☐ ☐ ☐

BRGS School Development Plan — AREAS FOR DEVELOPMENT

Meeting(s) of .... Date(s) ....

or

Submission from (Individual's name) .... Date ....

Number of item in Checklist	Detailed descriptions of the developments you would like to see	Year of Implementation

3   The content of school development plan (SDP)

Chapters One and Two described the development plan for the whole school as being a summary of the separate plans covering the core and support elements and explained the process by which

CORE ELEMENTS	SUPPORT ELEMENTS
Curriculum and curriculum development	Physical resources
Human resources	Pupil roll and marketing
Pupil welfare and pastoral care	Management structures and approaches
	Monitoring and evaluation mechanisms
	Financial resources

the plan should be created and operationalised. This chapter examines each of the elements on page 40 separately and guidance is given on the key components of each of them.

The process of producing a plan for implementation is common to both types of element and to whole school development planning. It involves:

- Reviewing the existing position;
- Stating the aims for that element (in relation to whole school aims);
- Specifying objectives, targets and indicators of success;
- Generating of alternative strategies;
- Prioritising in the short, medium and long term;
- Choosing between alternatives in the decision-making process.

Before detailed work can begin for each of the elements, the governors and the senior management team should consider their responses to the following:

- Who is *responsible* for drawing up the plan for each element?
- Who else *is* involved in drawing up the plan for each element?
- Who else *should be* involved in drawing up the plan for each element?
- What is the role of governors in drawing up plans for each element?

The importance of involving the school's partners in the preparation of the development plan, as well as in its implementation, is discussed in Chapter Four, while the sections which follow consider aspects of each of the separate core and support elements in turn.

Curriculum and curriculum development

National legislation (1986 *Education Act*) required that each LEA should have its own statement of curriculum policy which governors could use as a basis for reviewing their school aims and policy. Most governing bodies recognise the professional expertise of the staff so that the task of developing the curriculum policy is normally delegated to the head who, in turn, should involve the rest of the staff as appropriate. The curriculum development plan is then produced in order to turn that curriculum policy into action. While schools have always been involved in curriculum planning, the introduction of the National Curriculum brought about the need for specific National Curriculum Development Plans. There is, therefore, a short history of producing plans to meet curriculum development needs. It is possible, however, that the process of creating such a plan has not involved the staff in general but that the document has been produced by senior management in order to satisfy external requirements. We believe that if the plan is to be fully implemented at the classroom level then it should be constructed through a 'bottom up' process which involves all staff.

For each curricular area and for each cross-curricular theme there needs to be a group of people with responsibility for formulating a development plan. Such groups could include some or all of the staff affected (both teaching and non-teaching) and some governors. Curricular areas can no longer exist in isolation (as has been the tendency in secondary schools) so there must be a recognition of the need to involve staff from other areas. Similarly, a development plan for a cross-curricular theme must be drawn up by a cross-section of staff otherwise its priorities will be ignored at the implementation stage. Currently, governor involvement varies from school to school, depending on individuals' availability and on the management structures which are in place. In some schools they join working groups, in others they comment on drafts while, at the other extreme, some governors just rubber stamp the policy documents and plans which the head puts forward. Client groups such as pupils, parents and the local community, although largely neglected up to now, could take part in the development planning process and make a valuable contribution.

The aspects to be reviewed and the potential development and maintenance factors which might be included in the plan are very well covered in the second part of *Curriculum Guidance 3 — The Whole Curriculum* (National Curriculum Council 1990, obtainable from the National Curriculum Council, Albion Wharf, 25 Skeldergate, York YO1 2XL). The case studies in Chapters Six and Eight provide examplars and the following documentation may also prove useful:

- Flowchart and checklist on p44;
- Curriculum policy statement of the school;
- LEA curriculum policy documents;
- LEA guidance from advisers/inspectors/advisory teachers;
- Details of local staff development opportunities;
- National Curriculum documentation for each subject and cross-curricular theme;
- National Assessment and Testing documentation.

From each of the detailed subunit plans, a simple sheet of priorities would be put forward in order to build up the broader whole school curriculum development plan at the strategic/ tactical level. An example of a subunit plan and summary is found in Chapter Five. The job of bringing together the work of each of the subunits will probably fall to the head and deputy in a primary school and, in a secondary school, to the deputy head (curriculum) with a few other senior staff. Much of the consultation will already have taken place because all staff will have contributed at the earlier stages. However, if some priorities have to be disregarded or postponed, further consultation will be needed. It is likely that this will be because of financial or time constraints: it could be that subunits contradict each other or that priorities do not reflect the agreed whole school aims.

Just as with the subunits plans, the whole school curriculum development plan should be realistic rather than overambitious. The resulting targets may relate to particular curricular areas such as history or economic and industrial understanding or they may focus attention on broad issues right across the school such as differentiation or the recording of pupils' progress. This whole school plan will be at a more strategic level, stating areas for attention, rather than focusing on fine details, so readers would be referred to the subunit plans for further information. There would be some cross-referencing to other areas of the school development plan.

This overall curriculum development plan would then feed into the whole school development plan. Because of the centrality of the curriculum one would expect that the other aspects of the development plan (such as staff development as part of human resources) would support the identified curriculum priorities.

This process (either for subunits or for the whole school curriculum development plan) can now be summarised in Figure 3.1. This flowchart is accompanied by a checklist that acts as an *aide mémoire* for schools undertaking this process.

REVIEW THE
CURRICULUM

Within the school as well as
local and national pressures

Consider:
Breadth, balance, coherence,
progression
Curricular areas
Cross-curricular themes
Approaches to teaching and
learning
Assessment, record keeping
Planning.

CURRICULUM
DEVELOPMENT PLAN

Aims and policy
Maintenance factors and
developments: short, medium
and long term (with success
criteria)
Resource implications (including
staffing)

PRIORITIES

To whole school development
plan

Checklist

● Who is involved in and who
is responsible for subunit
plans (e.g. for the curricular
areas)?
● How do these curricular
areas develop their plans?
● How do the curricular
subunit plans feed into the
whole school curriculum
development plan?
● Who is responsible for
drawing up the main plan?
● Does the curriculum and
curriculum development
plan take account of present
and forthcoming national
and local policies and
legislation?
● Does the curriculum and
curriculum development
plan provide for continuity,
equality of opportunity, a
range of experiences and
cater for individual need?
● Who determines priorities?
● How are the governors
involved?
● Do the governors receive
this plan before the
budgetary process starts?
● Who is responsible for
overseeing the
implementation of this plan?

Figure 3.1   Core element: curriculum and curriculum development

Human resources

Staffing costs make up by far the largest part of a school's budget
so this is the area of expenditure which offers the greatest
potential for creativity and flexibility. It is therefore important to
plan deployment and development (and, hence, expenditure)
carefully in order to ensure maximum effectiveness. This applies
to both teaching and non-teaching staff and may extend to a

consideration of the use of volunteers and of support from external agencies.

A review of human resources will provide data to highlight the existing position in terms of roles, responsibilities and expertise. It will be necessary to review the number of staff, both teaching and non-teaching, and the nature of their contracts. There should also be an awareness of the availability of trainee teachers and the potential for attracting and utilising others undergoing work placements such as nursery nurses and laboratory technicians. There will be a need to review staff development to date and, bearing in mind confidentiality, to highlight outstanding priorities from the appraisal process.

Knowledge of teacher supply, in terms of quality and quantity, will inform recruitment policies and succession planning. The appointments procedure may need reviewing and revising now that schools have wider responsibility for staffing. The school's policy on employees' pay and conditions should be regularly reviewed to ensure that it reflects current legislation, provides clear guidelines, and does not disadvantage certain groups. This policy is especially important now that schools have much greater freedom to determine the nature of employees' contracts and the levels of remuneration. Alongside this, the governors and senior management must check that disciplinary procedures are in line with current legislation. There may also be a review of the school's equal opportunities policy to ensure that it can be applied to staff as well as to pupils.

The school's staff are there to serve the other aspects of the school's activities such as to deliver the curriculum, to provide pastoral care, and to provide a safe, pleasing environment. Staffing must, therefore, be 'needs-led' rather than 'supply-led'. Needs will be identified by collecting information from other reviews and plans (especially regarding the curriculum). For example, the curricular review may indicate the need for more expertise in music or for more science teachers. Priorities arising from the Physical Resources Development Plan may suggest the need to employ a 'handyman'. The Pupil Welfare Development Plan may point to a lack of pastoral continuity as pupils move through the age range. There may be a need right across all areas to develop particular common skills which are gaining in importance at subunit level, such as budgeting, handling meetings or relating with external organisations. Whole school needs, such as to increase all staff's knowledge and understanding of marketing, appraisal or disciplinary procedures may also become evident.

Having considered the existing position and the future needs, it will be possible to highlight gaps in provision in terms of policies, personnel or development needs. The planning process will then consider ways of meeting these needs. It may be necessary to redevelop aims and policies, but, if the existing ones are still appropriate, the plan will just focus on strategies for communicating policies to staff and on prioritising the activities required to realise the school's aims. Some possible aspects of the human resources development plan are considered below.

Many schools are now reconsidering *staffing levels* and the desirable ratio of teaching to non-teaching staff, full to part-time staff, and permanent to temporary staff. There may be different views in different parts of the school and the whole school plan can allow for variety. Careful long term planning is important here because of contractual and motivational factors.

A review of roles and responsibilities may have highlighted the need to have *job descriptions* which are structured in terms of specific expectations, rather than generalisations. Although the focus of teacher appraisal is on development, the individual's role needs to be more precisely defined than in the past if there is to be any meaningful discussion of progress and development. The formulation of these requires discussion and negotiation with the individual and probably with other colleagues so it takes considerable time. If a school feels that current job descriptions are inadequate, up to two years could be allowed to carry out the redefinition process across all staff. The job descriptions for all personnel should be made available to all staff and governors so that responsibilities are clear.

It is important that all those who work in the school feel that their own *development needs* are being met. Such a commitment by the school may be part of the mission statement: '. . . so that each individual can achieve his or her full potential . . .'. The school will probably have a system of discussing individual needs and strengths, especially with the teaching staff. This has usually evolved from a system of informal staff development discussions into a more structured process of appraisal. While the Human Resources Development Plan will involve the maintenance or further development of such a process, many schools may now wish to consider the extent to which such processes should apply to non-teaching staff. Formal or informal staff development for nursery nurses, technicians, caretakers and so on has often been neglected in recent years. However, if these staff are to be fully effective and committed to the school, they should be involved in developments, given responsibility and given the opportunity to attend meetings and courses which will allow them to be informed and able to contribute to the achievement of the school's aims.

Most schools have recognised the importance of assisting governors with their development needs but there may be scope for greater effectiveness in this area. Chapter Four describes how governors can interface with the staff in order to understand the major issues facing the school. When determining ways of meeting identified development needs, it should be remembered that they can be satisfied in a wide variety of ways such as reading, work-shadowing, or delegation — not necessarily just by attendance at courses.

Human resource development plans will support the other areas of the school, either curricular, management, or administrative. They will incorporate recruitment (or loss of staff), training and deployment at curricular or year group level and at the level of the whole school. The whole school plan will incorporate priorities from subgroups and will also include plans for whole school issues such as appraisal, while taking account of the governors' policies. When planning for this element, useful documents would be:

- Existing job descriptions;
- The governors' pay policy;
- The staff development policy;
- Appraisal policies;
- The equal opportunities policy of the school and LEA;
- *Teachers' Pay and Conditions Act* and circular;
- Guides to pay and conditions as produced by the teachers' associations;
- Current information on grants for staff development (eg GEST for LMS schools and SPG(D) for GM schools); and
- A Pay Policy (Managing Schools Today Vol 1 Nos 3 and 4 1991).

The planning process for this element is summarised in Figure 3.2 with a checklist as an *aide mémoire* for the various partners involved.

Pupil welfare and pastoral care

The central function of the school is to provide for the effective education of the pupils. As well as the overt curricular provision, it is necessary to focus on aspects of the hidden curriculum such as the way in which pupils are grouped and supported. In most schools overall responsibility for co-ordinating pupil welfare and pastoral care will be delegated to a senior member of staff such as the deputy head of a primary school or the deputy head (pastoral)

REVIEW HUMAN RESOURCES

Staffing structures (teaching and
non-teaching)
Roles and responsibilities
Staff development — current
policies

IDENTIFY NEEDS

from: Curriculum review
      Other school reviews

HIGHLIGHT GAPS

STAFF DEVELOPMENT PLAN

(dealing with appraisal, INSET,
recruitment and deployment)

Aims and policy
Individual and corporate needs
and plans
Maintenance factors and
developments: short, medium
and long-term (with success
criteria)
Resource implications

PRIORITIES

To whole school development
plan

Checklist

- Who oversees this element
  of the school's activity?
- Does the human resource
  plan refer to all staff, rather
  than just teachers?
- Who is responsible for
  recruitment, induction and
  retention?
- Are there opportunities for
  staff to accept real
  responsibilities?
- Who is responsible for staff
  development?
- How are individual, group
  and whole school
  development needs
  determined?
- Who determines priorities?
- Do all staff have job
  descriptions?
- How is success given
  recognition?
- Does the school have a pay
  policy which covers all staff?
- Does the school have a staff
  grievance procedure?
- How are the governors
  involved?
- Who is responsible for
  overseeing the
  implementation of policy
  and plans within this
  element?

Figure 3.2   Core element: human resources

in a secondary school. He or she would work closely with those responsible for sections of the school (such as infant/junior, lower/upper) or for year groups. At both whole school and year group level there must be extensive involvement of all other staff and partners such as pupils, parents and the appropriate support services. It is likely that sections of the school or year groups would develop specific plans (for example, covering interphase links) and that there would be whole school policies or issues permeating all age groups (for example, concerning rewards and sanctions). As with the curriculum development plan, it would probably then be the role of the deputy head or a senior management team to draw up a whole school plan for this element, bearing in mind the school aims. Working groups may find the following useful:

- Flowchart and checklist on page 53;
- The equal opportunities policy of the school and LEA;
- The governors' policy on pupil discipline and exclusion;
- LEA guidance from advisers or inspectors;
- Information from LEA or independent support services; and
- The Elton Report.

A wide variety of issues will need to be considered within this element. Plans will incorporate maintenance, development and implementation of the following, which are also examined in the sections below:

- Pupil grouping;
- Staff roles and responsibilities;
- Pastoral and hidden curriculum;
- Equal opportunities;
- Positive discipline/rewards and sanctions;
- Reporting, parental links and homework;
- Interschool links;
- Support services; and
- Community links.

Pupil grouping

Most primary schools have, traditionally, grouped pupils according to age although, for various reasons, many have adopted vertical grouping. As parents become more aware of their children's level of attainment within the national curriculum subjects, there will be increasing pressure placed on some teachers to explain how a pupil's individual needs are being met within the class, whether it is an age group or vertically grouped class.

Increasingly, pupils will be grouped using a pattern which approximates to their national curriculum level. Whichever approach is used, it will be necessary to communicate its effectiveness to parents.

Secondary schools usually group pupils into mixed ability classes or broad bands for registration and pastoral purposes but then a wide variety of patterns will come into operation for the traditional areas of curriculum delivery. Pupils may be streamed for one subject, banded for another and taught in mixed ability groups for another. However, desired flexibility may be compromised by timetable constraints. The development plan may consider that the curriculum should drive resources so that the timetable must be loosened up to allow a variety of pupil grouping approaches. Larger schools will have to consider how (or whether) to place registration groups into larger groups such as houses or years.

Staff roles and responsibilities

Primary schools encourage an holistic view of a child's development by placing both curricular and pastoral responsibility in the hands of one person: the class teacher. Coordination across a section of the school, for example by the teacher responsible for the early years, will also place emphasis on the whole child, rather than just on the curriculum or on rewards and sanctions. In a large school pupils will always fall conveniently into year groups according to their age. However, many secondary schools are abandoning the position of Head of Year and placing greater emphasis on the pastoral role of the form tutor and on the responsibilities of all teachers for the discipline and care of pupils, reflecting the holistic primary model. If major reorganisation of school structures is imminent, then this area of roles and responsibilities will need to be examined. It may be desirable to consider the rotation of certain roles in order to offer staff development opportunities and to allow pupils to experience a programme of pastoral care which is built up over time by blending the best ideas of a variety of staff.

Pastoral and hidden curriculum

A lot of attention is given to the overt curriculum, especially to 'subject areas'. If there is an expectation that class teachers will carry out certain other activities (which could constitute a pastoral curriculum) with their groups, for example at the beginning of the school day, then the school may wish to review the coherence and progression of this provision. At any time when the pupils are involved in school activities they are exposed to hidden messages and planning may be needed to ensure that these are in line with school policy. For example, staff must not convey any discriminatory messages or attempt to influence pupils politically. The hidden curriculum must be in line with the school's mission statement and policies.

Equal opportunities

Every school should have an equal opportunities policy. The development plan may include the process of revising or implementing this and, if so, managers must consider how the policy can be agreed, applicable to all, in line with legislation and workable.

Positive discipline/rewards and sanctions

There may be a need to review existing practice in this area in order to establish strengths and weaknesses. A consistent approach should be developed so that pupils know what to expect under certain circumstances. Many schools have already considered this topic over the last few years because central government funding has been available. If that is the case, a school's development plan may focus on the evaluation of the work carried out so far in order to examine its impact.

Reporting, parental links and homework

The partnership with parents is a very important aspect of the school's relationships with its clients. It encompasses a great many areas of activity and schools may find the following list useful:

- Written home–school communications;
- Parents' evenings and open days/evenings;
- School productions;
- Voluntary help in school;
- Fund raising; and
- Support and information about homework.

Reviewing and planning in this area lends itself particularly well to parent and pupil involvement. It could be the starting point for their wider involvement in school development planning. The quality of both the planning process and the subsequent activities may be enhanced by the designation of a member of staff to be responsible for home–school liaison.

When reviewing the reporting procedures, the school must take account of the national legislation but, at the same time, all communications must meet the requirements of the parents, as the clients. Schools may need to plan briefing sessions and explanatory documents as well as the actual report. Parents have differing commitments, both during the school day and in the evening. It can be very beneficial to the home–school partnership if these commitments are taken into account, where possible, when planning activities which should involve parents. Caution is needed, however, because excessive time demands on staff, for example in terms of extra meetings or the preparation of lengthy reports, will be counterproductive if the pupils' curricular experiences suffer through staff stress.

Interschool links

Most schools now devote some of their time to easing the transfer between one phase of schooling and another, although this may be a very limited system comprising one visit to the receiving school. Curriculum continuity is increasingly receiving attention but many schools could smooth the transition by examining approaches to teaching and learning and to the pattern of a child's day. Schools can join official clusters and consortia or they can create informal networks. There are many benefits to be gained from interschool links although some schools are now less willing to share ideas with others with whom they may to have to compete for pupils.

Support services

Increasingly schools can opt to buy in certain support services from a variety of sources or can provide the necessary support internally. The existing nature and level of support may have evolved in a piecemeal manner over time and the picture may be unclear. A thorough review of provision and need in this area will help schools to plan the most effective (which is not always the cheapest) way forward for the future. It will be necessary to establish and develop policies and suitable staff. The use of volunteers, as well as official agencies and the school's own staff, may be considered.

Community links

Another area which is increasingly being considered by schools is the relationship with the community. Unfortunately, developments are often taking place in an *ad hoc* way, rather than as part of coherent strategy. It is important to coordinate external relationships otherwise staff will be covering the same ground and may be trying to build up conflicting projects. If the school wishes

REVIEW THE SYSTEM OF PUPIL WELFARE AND PASTORAL CARE

Pupil grouping
Staff roles and responsibilities
Pastoral and hidden curriculum
Equal opportunities
Positive discipline/rewards and
  sanctions
Reporting, parental links and
  homework
Inter-school links
Support services
Community links

Checklist

- Who is, and who should be, involved in a review of this element?
- Who is, and who should be, involved in building up the plan?
- Who determines priorities?
- Who is responsible for overseeing the implementation of the plan?
- How are the governors involved?

PASTORAL DEVELOPMENT PLAN

Aims and policy
Maintenance factors and
  developments: short, medium
  and long term (with success
  criteria)
Resource implications

PRIORITIES

To whole school development
  plan

Figure 3.3 Core element: pupil welfare and pastoral care

to benefit from local industry and the local community, thought must be given as to what the school can provide in return. It may be better to have a 'slow creep' approach in this area in order to build trust.

The process of building up a development plan for pupil welfare and pastoral care is summarised in Figure 3.3 with a checklist that should help those undertaking this process.

Physical resources

A property management plan is essential now that schools are responsible for much of the day-to-day maintenance of the premises or, indeed, in the case of grant maintained schools, for all aspects of site management. Some projects will be expensive and so this plan should extend forward over several years, allowing for a phased or rolling programme of maintenance and development. If expenditure is put off now or is allowed to 'bunch' in certain years, there could be a detrimental effect on the future provision of curricular materials and staffing. Property management is an element of the school's activity to which governors and parents would be very likely to contribute as they may have wider expertise than the staff. Caretakers/site managers need to be involved so that they can supply information and so that they are motivated to be proactive and effective in their roles.

The review will need to consider each of the following:

- The distribution of responsibilities for repairs and maintenance, a pattern which is likely to change from time to time in LEA schools;
- Regular monitoring reports which will highlight the condition of the premises and the running costs, for example for energy and telephone usage;
- The availability of space in which to carry out the educational and support activities associated with the school, for example, the utilisation of classrooms, sports facilities, resource areas and other space, including office and staff accommodation, facilities for the caretaker, for storage and for school meals;
- Other elements of the school's activity in order to highlight specific needs, for example the need for more lockers or for new workstations for technology;
- Access for parents and for the disabled;
- The continued appropriateness of existing plans in the form of the current rolling programme of repair, maintenance and

refurbishment (as detailed in the previous year's development plan);
- The nature and effectiveness of contracts — so that possible
  alterations to specifications or contractors can be planned
  and negotiated;
- Building proposals from the LEA or diocese (for voluntary
  aided schools) — in order to incorporate building projects
  within the plan (or, in the case of GM schools, available
  expertise in estimating and knowledge of DES bidding
  procedures);
- The governors' statutory responsibilities for health and safety;
- Current Local Authority policies in relation to public
  buildings.

Those reviewing and planning in this area may need to take
professional advice on complex technical matters. This will
normally involve consultancy fees. In most schools, many new
projects will be identified and there will always be essential
repairs and maintenance. Before final decisions are made it will be
necessary to take account of any help which may be available from
outside the school. For example, there may be specific grants
available for a particular project which was not the school's
highest priority and it may be sensible to initiate such a project
while funding is available.

It is probable that there will be wide ranging needs to be met
within this element. Those who are responsible for choosing
between the various alternative projects should not act on whims
or choose projects which reflect their own individual preferences.
They should have a very precise set of criteria on which to base
decisions. They will need to be aware of their statutory
responsibilities for providing pupils with curriculum opportunities and their health and safety obligations.

This process of reviewing and planning is shown in Figure 3.4
which is accompanied by a checklist to assist those planning the
management of the school's physical resources.

Pupil roll and marketing

Now that the major part of a school's income is determined by the
pupil roll, it is more important than ever before to manage this
area well. Schools have always marketed themselves in some way,
even if only through relationships with parents when they visited
the school but, because of increased parental choice and
pupil-driven funding, a thorough review may be appropriate. A
strategic view of trends in overall pupil roll is needed in order to

```
┌─────────────────────────────────┐
│      REVIEW PHYSICAL            │
│        RESOURCES               │
│                                │
│ Review          Consider:      │
│ aspects:        Occupancy      │
│ Rooms             rate         │
│ Other indoor    Suitability    │
│   space         Access         │
│ Outdoor space   Furniture      │
│                   Fittings     │
│ Contracts:      General        │
│ Grounds           maintenance  │
│ Maintenance     Minor          │
│ Cleaning          alterations  │
│ Catering        Major          │
│                   alterations  │
│                 Efficiency and │
│                   effectiveness│
└─────────────────────────────────┘
```

```
┌─────────────────────────────────┐
│   PHYSICAL RESOURCES           │
│   DEVELOPMENT PLAN             │
│                                │
│ Aims and policy                │
│ Maintenance factors and        │
│   developments: short, medium  │
│   and long term (with success  │
│   criteria)                    │
│ Resource implications          │
└─────────────────────────────────┘
```

```
┌─────────────────────────────────┐
│         PRIORITIES             │
│ To whole school development     │
│   plan                         │
└─────────────────────────────────┘
```

Checklist

- Does the school have a property management plan and how does it fit into the overall planning cycle?
- Who is responsible for and who is involved in drawing up the plan?
- Does the planning process draw on information from parents, pupils, teaching staff, non-teaching staff and governors?
- Does the planning process allow for the incorporation of information about priorities from other elements of the school development plan?
- What is the timescale for the construction of this property management plan?
- Does the plan take account of short, medium and long term needs?
- How are the governors involved?

Figure 3.4   Support element: physical resources

plan all aspects of educational provision. It will also highlight fluctuating intakes, falling rolls or excessive demand for places. All of these will need a management response. In addition to this strategic view, areas of the school will need more detailed information, for example concerning whether pupils are likely to leave or join at certain ages or whether, in a secondary school, pupils are likely to opt for certain courses, especially post-16 (where the flexibility and choice is greater).

Information about the pupil roll is the central factor in the planning process because of its link with the budget of the school. The existence of the formula funding mechanism means that it is essential, initially, to maintain the pupil base and then, if appropriate, to seek ways to expand it for the long term survival of the school. The management of the pupil roll is achieved through the marketing process.

All schools have reputations and those reputations have to be managed. This area of reputation management or marketing is often misinterpreted as simply 'advertising' yet all schools must adopt a very proactive management stance because even the most popular school has to maintain its reputation and guard against complacency. The fundamental accountability and responsibility relationship of a school to its clients should be met within a marketing framework of effective communication with those clients.

An effective marketing policy enables the school to achieve this. Although more detailed issues will be examined at subunit level, most of the planning in this area will take place at the whole school level. It is quite possible that one person will be given overall responsibility for this element and that the work will be coordinated by a marketing group representing a cross-section of the staff, governors and the wider partners. However, all those who are associated with the school must understand their role as its ambassadors.

Schools need to consider the extent to which they work through, in a coordinated way, the stages in the marketing process as shown in Figure 3.5.

For further information on marketing schools the reader is referred to Davies and Ellison (1991) and Devlin and Knight (1990). Also, Figure 3.6 and its checklist may be useful as an *aide mémoire* when planning the management of the pupil roll and the marketing strategy.

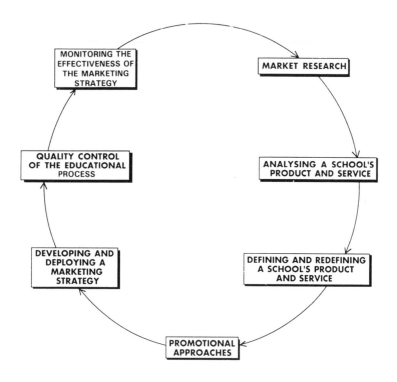

Figure 3.5: Marketing cycle (Davies and Ellison 1991, p37)

REVIEW PUPIL ROLL

Profile of present and future roll
   by age group
Information regarding ability
Location (catchment/not), local
   pupils going elsewhere

REVIEW MARKETING

Identify clients' wants, needs
   and their perceptions of the
   school
Review the product and service
   offered
Review the marketing process

**MARKETING
DEVELOPMENT PLAN**

Aims and policy
Maintenance factors and
   developments: short, medium
   and long term (with success
   criteria)
Resource implications

PRIORITIES

To whole school development
plan

Checklist

- Does the school have a
  strategy for managing its
  reputation?
- Who is responsible for
  managing the school's
  reputation? Is there a
  marketing committee?
- Is there a clear view of the
  profile of actual and
  potential pupil roll?
- Is there a clear process for
  identifying the clients and
  their needs and the school's
  strengths and weaknesses?
- Is there a clear view of what
  the school is offering?
- What are the resource
  implications of the
  marketing policy?
- Are all staff aware of these
  aspects of reputation
  management?
- How are the governors
  involved?

Figure 3.6   Support element: pupil roll and marketing

Management structures and approaches

Efficient and effective management structures are among the key factors needed for a successful school. Procedures must be in place for sharing out responsibilities and for ensuring effective communication and decision-making. A review in this area would need to involve a wide range of the school's partners and should take account of the structures at all levels and in all areas, for example governors, teaching staff, non-teaching staff, pupils and parents, including the links between the various groups.

The participation by the school's partners in the management of the school is discussed in more detail in Chapter Four but it is possible to outline here some of the areas to be considered.

1. *The structure and composition of decision-making groups* may require adjustment. Changes in the school, arising from a variety of factors, could mean that existing decision-making groups are no longer effective. For example, they may be very narrow in their composition so that cross-curricular and cross-age range continuity are affected. Thus, a review of this area would be needed.
2. *The degrees of delegation to different partners* may need to be altered in order to spread the workload, motivate staff and facilitate professional development.
3. *The extent of consultation* prior to decision-making may need widening. Previously, many staff have had no involvement and it is quite possible that the school's wider partners have had little opportunity for input.

Poor communication between the different partners is a common problem in all organisations, including schools. Even those who have recently reviewed and revised their procedures will still have their critics. It is important, therefore, to review this particular area regularly and to consider carefully the costs and benefits of any proposed modifications. Although good communication is vital to the school's success, it can be very expensive in terms of staff time and of materials.

A review of administrative functions should be carried out at regular intervals as it is quite likely that many of these are undertaken by teachers who have skills which could be better used in other areas, such as in curriculum planning and delivery. Examples are seen such as heads or deputy heads collating and stapling newsletters. It may be more effective to delegate decisions on the use of support staff to subunits within the school. A review of management information systems may indicate that the computerised system (where available) is not being used to its

REVIEW MANAGEMENT STRUCTURES AND APPROACHES

Review aspects:	Consider:
Management structures and relationships:	Individual and team roles Responsibilities including governors and external/boundary relations
Communications: up down across oral written	Involving staff, governors, pupils, parents, support services, other schools/colleges, industry/commerce, community, media
Administration:	Roles and responsibilities Management information systems

Checklist

- Is the existing management structure clear?
- Is the existing management structure in need of review?
- Do individuals and teams have clear responsibilities and objectives? Are there opportunities for delegation of responsibility so that staff can become involved and develop their expertise?
- Who makes decisions? Do decision makers have enough time?
- How is change initiated? What are the mechanisms for implementation?
- Will the structure have to change again or is it flexible enough to meet changing needs?
- Are communications between the partners adequate or excessive, effective or poorly thought out?
- What are the implications for training needs of any plans to improve the effectiveness of the management structure?

MANAGEMENT DEVELOPMENT PLAN

Aims and policy
Maintenance factors and developments: short, medium and long term (with success criteria)
Resource implications

PRIORITIES

To whole school development plan

Figure 3.7 Support element: management structures and approaches

maximum potential, indicating a training need. There may be a need to widen access to the software through additional terminals. Schools that do not have one of the sophisticated computer-based school management systems may consider the use of standard packages or generic facilities such as spreadsheets. However, there can be a lot of duplication of effort (for example in entering pupil data) when software packages do not interrelate.

Having reviewed the issues which fall within this element, it is then possible to plan the way forward. If changes to decision-making structures are needed, models can be drawn up for discussion amongst the staff and with the school's wider partners. As well as planning the actual changes themselves, it will be necessary to plan associated staff development and to plan the communication of new structures, for example through awareness-raising sessions.

This process is summarised in Figure 3.7 with a checklist to act as an *aide mémoire*.

Monitoring and evaluation mechanisms

The process of evaluation is one of the stages in the management cycle as described in Chapter Two. The desired nature of evaluation and the mechanisms to be used in the school can be considered as one of the support elements within the school development plan. Several questions must be considered in order to clarify responsibilities and procedures.

A review should consider *why* the school is monitoring and evaluating its activities. This will be in order to ensure a quality dimension but will also be to fulfil statutory obligations.

What will be monitored and evaluated? Certain elements of activity must be monitored regularly by every school. These would include such varied activities as the spending of the budget against the predicted income budget, and the achievement of pupils in relation to national norms and expectations. Evaluation, a much more complex process, could be used to relate expenditure on a new maths scheme to levels of achievement in that area. However, it is appropriate to consider whether each element of the school's activity should be evaluated separately or whether there should be a more holistic view which takes account of interrelated factors. Is it the inputs to the school, or its educational processes or some measure of outputs that is being examined? These models can be seen if we view a school as an organisation having inputs which are combined together through a process in order to achieve outputs as follows:

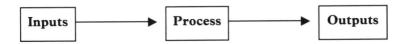

Evaluation can be carried out at any or all of these three points. The danger is that they are very often confused and individuals are unclear which form of evaluation is being used.

Is the use of delegated funds being evaluated (the inputs) or the teaching of the National Curriculum (the process) or the results of testing at one of the key stages (the outputs)? Focusing on one to the exclusion of the others leads to a distorted view of the school. What is needed is a value added approach where increased control over resources, through delegated finance, can be seen to affect the learning process and increase the learning outcomes. While monitoring and evaluation should focus on helping the school to increase the quality of student outcomes, the evidence can only be seen in context if the first two, inputs and process, are considered in parallel.

Who will carry out the monitoring and evaluation? Monitoring will normally be carried out by those who are very close to the activity. This will therefore involve teaching and non-teaching staff and, perhaps, even the pupils and parents. There is a tendency to expect thorough evaluation to be carried out by inspectors but, as schools become self-managing institutions, this will increasingly become an internal process.

How and when will it take place? Monitoring is an ongoing process of data collection which is reported at regular intervals, such as monthly, termly or annually, depending on the audience. Although a brief review is carried out during or after most activities, such as a lesson or an assembly, more in-depth evaluation has, until recently, been less frequent or indeed, has been non-existent. Now that schools have greater freedom in the use of resources and are more accountable to their clients, annual evaluation of activities will become the norm. This will involve a consideration of resource use in relation to outcomes.

What is the nature of the process? What criteria or *performance indicators* will be used? Various lists of possible indicators have been produced, especially in relation to the evaluation of self-managing schools. The most valuable indicators are those which are determined during the development planning process by the school for its own improvement. For example, a target set as part of the property development plan could be that each pupil should have a locker by a certain date.

What *level of achievement* is acceptable? In relation to the above performance indicator concerning lockers, the ideal would be to achieve the target, but it may be considered acceptable to achieve 80 per cent success within the timescale. Under what circumstances will remedial action be needed? School managers need an indication of what is deemed to be unsatisfactory progress towards a target so that they can ask questions which will help to rectify the situation. For example, a head of department or curriculum coordinator will need to intervene quickly if a teacher is not maintaining accurate records of pupil progress after four weeks of a new term.

What is the *audience* for the final report? The format and language should be considered in relation to the receivers' level of understanding in that area. A monthly monitoring report on the school's budget to the finance committee may be very different from one which is given to a member of staff with responsibility for a curricular area.

It is unlikely that there will be a major review of monitoring, evaluation and reporting each year. Once the procedures have been considered, revised and operationalised, it will normally be at least three years before further modifications are required.

The flowchart and checklist in Figure 3.8 summarise the stages of reviewing and planning for this element of the school's activity.

Financial resources

While various groups are preparing development plans for the other core and support elements, a group must work on the financial plan. This process is described in Chapter Two but is also mentioned here to emphasise the close liaison which is required between this group and those working on the plans for the other elements. The group should:

- Review the pattern of income and expenditure in the current year;
- Consider the level of the ongoing expenses;
- Examine potential sources of income;
- Collect preliminary information about the likely expenditure needs in the various core and support elements;
- Predict the pattern of income and expenditure for three years; and
- Draw up draft budget plans for one year.

When the whole school development plan has been created, the

REVIEW MONITORING AND EVALUATION MECHANISMS	
Review aspects of:	**Consider:**
Monitoring	Why do it?
	Who does it?
Evaluation	What data is being collected?
Reporting	Timescales
	Time available
	Clear indicators for success
	The process
	How information is presented
	Who receives information?
	Of all core and support areas?
	External views

Checklist

- Who is responsible for overseeing monitoring, evaluation and reporting in the various core and support areas and for the school as a whole?
- Who carries out these activities?
- Is monitoring and evaluation planned? Does it relate to planned targets? Does it involve overall and focused reviews as necessary?
- Is time set aside for these activities?
- What are the other resource implications of monitoring and evaluation?
- Who receives the various reports?
- When was the last external inspection? How was the information used?
- Do monitoring and evaluation result in improvement? VE

MONITORING AND EVALUATION DEVELOPMENT PLAN

Aims and policy
Maintenance factors and developments: short, medium and long term (with success criteria)
Resource implications

PRIORITIES

To whole school development plan

Figure 3.8 Support element: monitoring and evaluation mechanisms

resource implications will be examined and then the plan may be adjusted to take account of resource availability.

Conclusion

This chapter has sought to provide a framework for undertaking the necessary review and analysis of the key elements in the school development plan. While for administrative and management convenience they have been considered separately, the integrated nature of school development planning should not be forgotten. It is only when proposals for the individual elements have been collated that their significance can be effectively assessed and the totality of the plan put into practice. The way in which this can be achieved is demonstrated in the case studies in Chapters Six to Nine. The next chapter considers in detail the role of the various partners in the school development planning process.

References

Davies B and Ellison L, *Marketing the Secondary School*, Longman 1991
Devlin T and Knight B, *Public Relations and Marketing for Schools*, Longman 1990
Managing Schools Today Vol 1 Nos 3 and 4 1991

4 Managing the process — The role of governors, staff, parents and pupils in school development planning

The previous three chapters have established the nature and dimensions of school development planning. If a plan is to be successfully translated into action, attention must be given to the process by which decisions are made. This necessitates examining the role of the various partners in the school. It is also important to determine the sequence and timing of the planning process and of the subsequent reporting of progress.

In the past, governors and staff have usually operated separately while parents and pupils have had little involvement in determining priorities. Schools, whether within the LEA or grant maintained, now have a far wider range of responsibilities and are much more accountable to the communities which they serve. It is therefore important that the roles of governors and staff are clear and that they do not duplicate each other's activities. Parents and pupils, as the main clients and customers, have a significant contribution to make in designing the school development plan. The contributions of all these groups need to be integrated to develop a partnership and focus effort.

When discussing the role of the headteacher and governors, DES guidelines on LMS (Circular 7/88) state that:
'the headteacher will have a key role in helping the governing body to formulate a management plan for the school, and in securing its implementation with the collective support of the school's staff.'

The next section of this chapter examines the ways in which this partnership can be developed and extended to include parents and pupils in order to enhance the quality of school management and, hence, to provide effective education.

Policy formulation

Effective education is achieved by the implementation of planned activities which are in line with appropriate policies. Existing policies will need reviewing and, where necessary, revising. New policies may be required in areas where they do not already exist. Thus, the school development plan and the process of creating it may be informed by existing policies. On the other hand, the plan may identify policy development as a priority for the year in question.

When considering the area of policy making, the school must organise a process (introduced on page 8) involving four activities: policy generation, policy approval, policy implementation, and policy administration. The initial activity, policy generation, involves the creation of the various policies for the school, for example regarding pupil admissions or curriculum. The policy approval dimension of the process takes place when the final decision is made to implement the policies which have been developed. Policy implementation is the tactical activity of translating policy aims and decisions into practice through the school development plan. The recording of information and similar activities provides the policy administration function.

There is no simple strategy which can be used to determine levels and patterns of participation and involvement that would be appropriate for every school: each school must develop its own way of working. Do governors merely approve the policies that are put before them or are they involved in some of the initial discussions which set the parameters for the decision-making process? How is the changing role of governors being accepted and implemented within the school? Staff are unlikely to be motivated if they are simply carrying out instructions rather than developing a sense of ownership through being involved in the design and generation of policies within the school. Policy administration should largely be carried out by support staff therefore it may be helpful to consider some involvement at earlier stages so that they understand the background to their work.

While other parts of this book look at the technical aspects of school development planning, the subsections which follow analyse the roles of the various partners in policy development and in its implementation through the development plan.

1.   The role of governors

When examining the role of governors in designing and implementing the school development plan, three factors must be considered in order to establish an effective working relationship with the school.

(a)   If governors are to take a strategic role they need to develop a broader and deeper understanding of their school.

(b)   Governors should concentrate on broad policy issues and not on the detailed day-to-day running of the school.

(c)   The most effective use has to be made of the limited time which governors can devote to the school.

It is undesirable and impractical for the governors to have more and more meetings, either full governors' meetings or subcommittees. Instead, to save time and avoid the duplication of effort, they should link to the internal committees in the school. Half termly progress review meetings could be organised at which staff or subgroups of staff would update the governors on policy developments to date in a particular area and engage them in a discussion as to the desirability and viability of the various options. This approach would have two purposes: firstly, it would integrate the governors with the internal school management; and secondly it would provide them with a broad information base on which to make decisions. Each review meeting would be about an hour long and would tackle just one issue, such as curriculum or marketing, with staff and governors together. This could be followed by a standard governors' meeting or a subcommittee meeting.

Although not all governors are able to attend all these 'one hour, one issue' meetings, this level of activity is necessary if the role of the governor is to be one of an informed partner in the relationship between staff, governors as representatives of the community and, where appropriate, the LEA. It is important that all governors should be involved, rather than just a subgroup, so that collectively they are aware of a range of issues and have an

informed view. Thus, with this information, the governing body
can take a broad policy approach which is appropriate to its
strategic management role.

2. The role of the senior management team

The headteacher and other members of the senior management
team are at the interface between governors and staff and are the
key players in the design and implementation of the school
development plan. They have the role of engaging the governors
in a strategic dialogue as to the aims of the school and how, in
broad terms, they might be achieved. This agenda will also
provide a list of performance indicators for the school and its
management so that checks can be made later to see if these have
been achieved. Governors are increasingly likely to use the extent
to which school development plan targets have been met as a
means of appraising the performance of the senior management
team.

The senior management team also has to develop appropriate
approaches to involve the staff of the school in the development
planning process. This is vital if staff are to be committed to
fulfilling the objectives of the plan. *Top down* approaches where
staff are merely informed of decisions are unlikely to motivate
them. Similarly *bottom up* approaches where the staff are given
little direction are unlikely to be successful. What is needed is an
integrated approach where the skills and experience of senior
management are used in working with governors to lay down the
basic framework and where staff make a significant contribution
within this framework. The headteacher and senior staff must
coordinate and manage this process as well as providing the
necessary leadership.

3. The role of staff

Good management practice would suggest that there should be
considerable staff involvement in the formulation of the school
development plan and in the associated resource decisions. The
term 'staff' is used here to include all those who work in the
school, whether in a teaching or a non-teaching capacity.

One of the main reasons for the move to Local Management of
Schools and Grant Maintained Status is the belief that when it
comes to decision-making, the closer the decision-maker is to the
final client or customer the better quality and more appropriate
will be the decision. Therefore, if decision-making is delegated
from LEAs to schools because they are closer to the children there
is a strong argument that this criterion should be applied within

the schools. Should delegation and participation in decision-making stop at the level of the governors and senior management team or is there a significant role for other staff in the school because they are in day-to-day contact with the children?

If staff are not to perceive school development plans as imposed documents, threatening accountability, they need to be involved in the planning and decision-making process. Involvement in the decision-making process will allow staff to feel committed to the proposed activities and to the means of achieving them. They should, therefore, be involved in determining needs, setting priorities, and making choices between those priorities. In terms of the policy stages listed on page 68, staff should contribute to policy generation as well as to policy implementation. The extent and organisation of this consultation and/or participation is for each school to determine and to make clear.

4.   The role of parents and pupils

An excellent example of involving pupils and parents in the school development planning process is provided by Bacup and Rawtenstall Grammar School's audit questionnaire (pages 25–39). The school found this to be a very constructive way of collecting contributions to the development planning process and it also highlighted parents' and pupils' priorities, information which tends to receive little formal attention in many schools. The reporting back on the items raised by the parents and pupils can provide a valuable form of accountability. This last point cannot be underestimated. If schools are to fulfil their basic mission of providing the highest quality education possible to their clients, it is vital that the clients themselves should be involved in the process and not just be passive recipients.

The annual school development planning cycle

Although, in this book, we suggest various elements which should be covered by a school development plan, we do not propose that each of these should be examined in great detail every year. In order to avoid work overload it may be necessary, especially in small schools, to prioritise the elements which will be considered each year, although certain elements (such as curriculum) would obviously be examined annually. Neither do we advocate the creation of permanent subcommittees for each element. In this section we examine some issues related to committee structures and outline a possible division of tasks across the whole school year.

One of the curses of the education system is that, when faced with a challenge or a problem, the solution is often seen to be the formation of committee to deal with it. There is a need to avoid the duplication of effort and the creation of numerous special committees. The development planning process should seek to harness the existing work that is being done in the school. Information concerning most of the elements of the plan is already available. Governors should not, either individually or in groups, replicate the work being done by staff but should draw on and build on that work.

Where subcommittees are established, they should, ideally, be in the form of team and task groups. Research shows that, rather than larger general discussion groups, the most effective groups comprise six to eight people who are focused on completing a specific task. These groups are not necessarily official subcommittees of the governing body so they can include the other partners in the educational process as appropriate. They are convened to perform a particular function, such as determining the coming year's budget or developing an equal opportunities policy. Once the task has been completed, the group is dissolved although, for continuity of experience, it might be desirable to have some of the members on a similar team in the future. Such a system enables a range of people to contribute to planning and prevents people from feeling that they cannot contribute in a particular area because it is someone else's permanent role.

The strategic responsibility of the governors and senior staff is to draw together the work of the subgroups in a coherent way to form a whole school plan. It was suggested earlier that, at various points in the school year, governors should be briefed on aspects of the plan's key elements so that they have the understanding to review the provision strategically and can plan appropriate action in consultation with the headteacher and senior staff.

Schools will need to establish a process that will enable governors to have sufficient time, for example before the submission of plans to the LEA, to consider policies and priorities with the advice and support of the headteacher and staff. Figure 4.1 shows when the various activities might take place during the school year.

Links with the LEA

In LEA schools the reporting and decision-making process has to meet the needs of both the school and of the LEA in formulating their policies. Officers will need to aggregate information from the schools within the authority to feed into the overall planning

---

Summer Term

Review: Pupil welfare and pastoral care

Physical resources

Pupil roll and marketing

Action: Governors to consider any areas for immediate attention or inclusion in next school development plan

Provisional staff development needs to LEA for GEST bidding

Implementation of new budget

Evaluation of previous year's budgetary process and outturn figures

---

Autumn Term

Review: Curriculum

Management structures

Human resources — deployment and development

Action: Consider data from any internal or external evaluation report

Draft school development plan to be formulated — LEA to receive details by the end of term in order to inform its planning process

Consider financial monitoring reports — check levels and vire as necessary

Budgetary review and forecasting for coming year

Spring Term

Review: Monitoring, evaluation and reporting procedures

Action: Determine final staffing and other resource levels

Provisional budget preparation

Agree final LMS budget with the LEA (either at the end of this term or the beginning of next)

LEA schools to submit development plan to the LEA

Make documents available to staff when agreed

Figure 4.1 Sequence of planning events

process. The LEA will also need specific information, especially concerning staff development needs and possible capital projects, from schools to assist in activities such as bidding for specific grants.

Grant maintained schools

These schools will obviously take on those aspects of financial and other planning previously undertaken by the LEA. The governors will have an increased role as they are responsible for the total management of the school, including the physical structure and the responsibility for all aspects of managing staff. They will have to fit their planning cycles to suit the information needs of the DES, for example regarding bids for special purpose grants, as well as to suit the needs of the school. Without the traditional form of LEA support, governors and the senior management teams of grant maintained schools will have to develop a long term strategic plan as well as the annual and three year planning view.

Conclusion

This chapter has highlighted some of the process and people dimensions of school development planning. It is important that schools pay as much attention to the way in which the plan is created as they do to its actual content. After approval, extensive communication and consultation will ensure that the plan is interpreted and implemented in a way which will lead to effective education for the pupils.

Reference

DES, *Education Reform Act: Local Management of Schools*, Circular 7/88, DES 1988

5 The format of the school development plan

A school development plan should be accessible to all the partners in the educational process. Its format must, therefore, be thought out carefully in order to ensure that these varied partners can understand and assimilate the information. This chapter will give some key points to consider when planning or evaluating the presentation of the document. It will then apply these points to different examples of practice. Finally we expand on the outline structure which was put forward on page 19, suggesting a format which will be used in the case study chapters.

Key characteristics

The whole school document should have a number of characteristics. Firstly, it should be *concise*, giving a brief synopsis of the school's plans and priorities. Further detail would be contained in other documents held elsewhere in the school. Secondly, it should be *understandable*. To ensure this, consideration should be given to the language and terminology, bearing in mind the audience. It should be possible to have the draft document scanned by a few representatives of the final audience. Thirdly, the content of the document should be *relevant*, providing the basic information which is needed by each of the school's partners. The document should be *usable*, both as a working document during implementation and as a progress record for monitoring and evaluation purposes. Finally, it should be *clear*, using high quality wordprocessing and copying.

Presentation

The form of presentation can be based mainly on text, mainly on graphics or a combination of both styles. It is important to be aware of the preferences of the school's partners as some people are 'put off' by text, preferring charts, tables and cycles. On the other hand, some people 'switch off' if they see flowcharts and cycles. If text is the main method of display, it is important to space the text so that it is easy to read. Headings and side headings will help the reader to see the structure of the document and to find specific sections as required. The use of lists will help to clarify points and priorities. Lists are also helpful when monitoring progress within the plan. Graphic presentation may take several forms, but the most useful in the overall school development plan would probably be flowcharts and simple charts or matrices. More detailed plans at subunit level may incorporate graphs. Bar charts and pie charts could be included but lend themselves more readily to use in monitoring and evaluation.

A combination of text and graphics may be appropriate. However, a school's priority should be to aim for clarity rather than attempt to incorporate as many presentational approaches as possible! An ideal combination (which we demonstrate in Chapters Seven and Nine) may be a contextual statement followed by an easy reference chart.

Examples

Most examples of existing good practice rely on a layout which is largely text. The plan from New Parks Community College is a good example of this type. We present here the outline whole school development plan for 1991/2 (Figure 5.1) without the supporting documentation such as detailed subunit plans and appendices. This is followed by a more detailed plan for one of the elements — curriculum support (Figure 5.2).

NEW PARKS

COMMUNITY COLLEGE

DEVELOPMENT PLAN

GRENCOAT ROAD
LEICESTER

PRINCIPAL: N.R. THOMPSON B.A., M.A.

MAY 1991

Figure 5.1   New Parks Community College whole school development
plan

DEVELOPMENT PLAN PROCESS

In line with the increasing demands made on schools and colleges, certain re-alignments in management and administration have evolved during the year. These include renegotiation of roles and responsibilities for the senior teachers, classification of the roles and responsibilities for the non-teaching staff and prioritisation of targets/projects for the vice principals. (Appendix A, B & D.) The management priorities are simply to ensure that communication is effective and to support staff within the College. In addition to this, it is our intention to prioritise time for linking with parents.

For 91/92 and for the next few years the main targets for the college have been agreed as "making the college more effective" by ensuring that the curriculum is "accessible and differentiated". The organisation of the college lends itself to enabling these targets to be identified and developed. The production of a shadow staffing structure has assisted in the discussion even though events have overtaken us and it is already out of date (Appendix C).

In line with the discussion and decision relating to development planning for the College, an integrated approach has been adopted. A separate Community Development Plan has not been written but priorities have been incorporated within the College plan.

The deliberations of the past year have been summarised in the following areas:

Curriculum
Curriculum Support
Support Curriculum
Financial Resources
Physical Resources
Community

These represent summary statements of the targets which have been identified and agreed upon for 91–94 and are related to the development plan priorities of "effectiveness, accessibility and differentiation".

COLLEGE — MISSION STATEMENT

In partnership with the community, New Parks Community College aims to equip students to be confident, responsible and well educated, so that they can fulfil positive roles in society."

We strive to achieve this by providing a just, stimulating, caring environment where excellence can develop through high quality learning experience based on individual needs and abilities.

CURRICULUM

Needs 91–94

Consolidate Keystage 3 in core subjects.
Continue KS 3 preparation for foundation subjects.
Plan KS 4 delivery — Curriculum and timetable structure, time allocation.
To improve Differentiation ⎫
To consider Accessibility ⎬ within the statutory, formal, informal
To consider Entitlement   ⎭ and community curriculum.
Continue development of recording and assessment procedures.

Priority Targets

Continue to develop links with Primary schools, employers and Colleges of
Further Education.
Plan Keystage 4 delivery.
Continue and expand work done on differentiation.
Recording and assessment procedures and develop reporting/links with
parents.
To evaluate Community Education and Youth Education Programme.

Timescale

Keystage 4 delivery to be decided by May 1992.
Other matters to be ongoing in the light of developments.

Involvement

Senior Management team
All staff
Governors
Management Committee
Students
Parents
Members of the Community

Methods/Approaches

Discussion and proposal through working groups, Heads of Department
meetings, Senior Management meetings, Departmental meetings, input
from Advisory staff and invited speakers, Governors' meeting, subcommittees, Management Committee and User groups.

Resource Implications

Mainly a question of time management — careful planning of meeting
cycle.
Development of differentiation will require some outlay on teaching
materials and may have implications for staffing and in-service work.

Consolidation of KS 3 and development of KS 4 will require extra
expenditure on teaching materials.

Staff Implications

Leading from any consideration of Keystage 4 will emerge a need to consider the present staffing imbalances and shortages. Assuming that the intake holds at its present level, and that the policy of the college is to use specialist teachers wherever possible there will be a need in 1992/3 for another Maths teachers, a History teacher and possibly a teacher of Modern Languages. Bearing in mind that we will probably have enough "bodies" numerically to cover our teaching commitment, the problem will have to be approached both from a short and long term view. That is to say that we will need to ensure that any curriculum or timetable proposals that we make can be accomplished satisfactorily with our present staff, while at the same time having a clear idea of what we are working towards, so that as staffing personnel changes we can make appropriate appointments or even think about re-training for existing (and likely to remain permanent) staff.

The establishment of a Community Arts Centre within the college may provide certain staffing flexibility within various departments within the College as teaching time may be able to be "bought in" to cover particular skills within the project.

Inset Requirements

Institutionally based inset with inputs from Senior staff, Advisors, and other members of staff with expertise in certain cases. Use of Inset days to allow discussion to take place in departmental and cross-curricular groups.

Development of links with Junior schools and F.E.

CURRICULUM SUPPORT

The Curriculum support team will build upon the developments of 1990/91. In 1991/92 the involvement of the department in the National Curriculum areas will be increased. Whilst still liaising with the Maths and Science departments, close liaison with the English, Humanities and Technology departments will take place. Through working together it is hoped that the National Curriculum will be made accessible to all students and especially to the regular 10% of students who have Special Needs. The creation of link teachers within all departments will facilitate this and also ensure a widening band of expertise throughout the college.

The Curriculum Support room will be further developed as a resource base with closer links with I.T. and the Library Resources areas. A general review and re-distribution of resources within departments will be undertaken and a purchasing policy investigated. Greater use of the support agencies and the strengthening of links with them will be pursued.

The testing to identify the specific needs of and progress made by students will become more formalised as will the monitoring of progress through programmes of study, assessment procedures and the pattern of meetings which will be established with the Pastoral Board, departments, students and parents.

Close links with the Primary Schools and Post 16 provisions will be maintained and improved.

There will continue to be a system of withdrawal and in-class support decided upon through consultation with staff and support agencies, the emphasis always being placed upon programmes of study which encourage access to the curriculum.

SUPPORT CURRICULUM

The Support Curriculum will continue to develop the skills which will enable all students to develop socially and have access to areas of the curriculum. In years 7, 8 and 9 this will be serviced through the Tacade programme and in years 10 and 11 through a case study approach leading to BTEC certification.

Consideration will be given to evaluating the existing programmes of study and to refining and developing the courses in order to meet the changing needs of our students in the rapidly changing society in which they live.

Emphasis will be placed on such matters as Equal Opportunities, Multi-Cultural Education, Careers, Economic and Industrial Awareness and Health Education. There will be continued involvement in Compact and Project Trident.

The course will also look at community aspects and through the students identify and expand the links through increased community involvement and a community service programme of study.

In-service requirements of staff will be identified and met through discussion and prioritising needs.

The support systems within the college will be evaluated and refined. Greater emphasis will be placed upon home and college links through the House system and procedures initiated to improve the service we offer to students and their families.

The college will continue to work closely with all the support agencies, strengthening links, sharing ideas and expertise in order to provide the caring and supportive environment the college aims to achieve.

COMMUNITY

TARGETS 91–94

1. Establishment of a Community Arts Centre within the College which encourages people from the local area in the local community to become involved in their own personal development.

2. To evolve a financial plan for the community provision of the College which reflects the decision making cycle for the College.

3. To develop further links within the community through a community service scheme.

4. Extend Community Education programme of formal and informal activities.

5. Develop and support the work with the under 5's and to establish a dedicated area for the use of the under 5's.

6. Develop and extend its work with the disadvantaged/unemployed, greater curriculum links with the statutory college curriculum.

7. Support work with aged and adults with special needs.

IN-SERVICE

Identify in-service requirements of full time, part time and voluntary staff and build it into the inset development plan for the College.

Identify a budget for in-service for community staff and involve the professional tutor in planning courses and identifying priorities for the college.

FINANCIAL RESOURCES

1991–92	1992–93	1993–94
Review of department allowances — W.F.'s and course development in the light of College and departmental development plan and the end of T.V.E.I.	Action priorities and policy ⟶	⟶
Consider provision for T.V.E.I. finances for consolidation into budget.	Consolidate T.V.E.I. into budget	
Make available funding for physical resource improvement included in this Development Plan.	⟶	
Review of depreciation of general fabric of the building and equipment in line with good standards of maintenance, health & safety and general enhancement of the learning environment.	⟶	
Careful monitoring of community delegated budget.		
Careful monitoring of caretaking/cleaning costs and lettings charges. Procedural refinements where necessary.	Action priorities	
Whole school project for electricity savings Nov–Feb and review.	Priorities for policy on use of electricity	
Investigate types and sources of sponsorship especially in the funding of prospectus and community newspaper.	⟶	Review charging policy
Review of charging policy.		
Support P.T.F.A. in fund raising and financing functions.	⟶	
	Major fund raising event Autumn 1992	

PHYSICAL RESOURCES

1991–92	1992–93	1993–94
Prepare for science accommodation shift to North building.	Science accommodation amalgamation	
Consider knock-on effect of above	Action re knock-on effect of science move	
Refurbishment of 2 toilets to cater for the disabled. Review security provision and procedures throughout the College. Fire door replacement.		
Flat roof renewal in rolling programme	⟶	⟶
Continue ongoing internal redecoration and furniture and furnishings replacement.	⟶	⟶
Ceiling renewal for north gym.		
Retarmacing of south yard ramp and delivery entrance of community building.		
Refurbishment of room 36 for multi-purpose usage.		
Provide some provision for student relaxation areas in each house.		
Consider and make available provision for Community Arts Workshop. Make available Technology Workshop.	Review usage of Community Arts Workshop	⟶
Consider proposals to fund building adaptation for the community building. Implement a strategy for improving the continual problem of litter on the campus.		

CURRICULUM SUPPORT DETAILED DEVELOPMENT PLAN
1991–1994

PRIORITY TARGETS

Making the Curriculum More Accessible 1991/92

To make the curriculum more accessible we need to have knowledge of all the subject programmes on the National Curriculum attainment targets.

The National Curriculum has started in English, Maths, Science, Technology and soon Humanities.

We shall continue targeting Science and also target English to develop differentiated teaching resources and methods in both areas.

In order to facilitate this, close contact with both departments with hard talking will take place. There will also be close contact with the English and Science advisers and S.E.N. area co-ordinator.

The achievements resulting from work with members of the Science and English departments need to be passed on to other members of the departments by meetings and discussions. This is essential for the programmes of study, developed to cover the fall-short and regular 10% of students who need S.N. help, to carry on successfully in the future. The creation of Link Teachers will also help ensure this.

Resources

The Curriculum Support Base will be further developed as a resource base with closer links with I.T. and Library Resource areas.

This year we will develop a Science area which will consist of samples of differentiated teaching materials such as text, hardware and software which shows ways to enhance the learning experience.

Contact will be made with the Library Loan Service for additional resources.

In-service time to be introduced to help individual teachers needs to develop materials and skills necessary to meet the needs of mixed ability teaching.

Curriculum Support base meetings will be arranged with the Science Department in the autumn term by which time the Science Area will be started.

Feedback on progress made in Science by the end of the autumn term including an Open Day of Curriculum Support Base with sharing of ideas.

Figure 5.2 Detailed curriculum support plan from New Parks Community College

Look at redistribution of resources within departments to meet the needs of all students e.g. money spent on tape records as alternative ways of recording information. Part of our policy will be that departments will share in the cost of resourcing differentiated teaching materials.

Testing to Identify Specific Needs of and Progress Made of Students

Close links with English Department on what tests are used, when and with whom, will be developed.

The importance of monitoring of methods of assessment, so that they can be evaluated will be attended to.

Mini reviews every half term for students with statements to be continued and also half term reviews on others with special needs.

Record files, including progress made, will be kept and made available on individual students with special needs. Regular feedback will create a closer link with staff involved. Also regular meetings with staff to discuss individual students' progress.

Clinic periods will be continued to encourage students to self-refer and staff to refer students who feel they have a special need.

Member of Curriculum Support Department will attend Pastoral meetings and be involved with home visits.

Tracking will also be employed to identify specific needs and progress made by students.

Primary School Liaison

Visits will continue to Primary Schools to help the transfer of students to secondary school.

Prospective intake students will be tested in their final year on their literacy skills.

Close links with primary school tutors to discuss special needs students.

Attendance of Annual Reviews of Statemented Students who will be attending N.P.C.C.

Staffing Structure

There are two full-time members of the curriculum support department. There have been additional hours tutors for statemented students and we hope this will continue.

Flexible withdrawal to continue. Groups of eight are envisaged for those with poor literacy skills (R.A. –9 below) on a comprehension self support basis. Also short stay groups (R.A. 9–10) on a half term basis for a blitz programme on raising reading level. This will involve close liaison with the English department.

Most of the support lessons will be with the Science and English departments. However support will also be given, where possible, in other areas, wherever the need is greatest.

There will be a strengthening of links and consultation with departments. Link teachers will be developed and regular meetings will take place. Departments will be encouraged to provide their own support provision with help and guidance from the Curriculum Support Department.

The Curriculum Support Department will be pro-active and there will be positive input into Head of Department and Department meetings.

A member of the Curriculum Support Department will attend as many other department meetings as possible. The needs of students will be discussed in these meetings.

There will be a continuation of links with the Special Needs Careers Officer and use made of "The Directory of Provision" which is concerned with opportunities for young people with special needs in further and community education. Close links with the post 16 Special Needs Advisory Service and the Rathbone Society.

Students

Screening of intake to identify reading and comprehension ages.

R.A. of 9–10 half term for blitz on reading.

R.A. 9–below for longer withdrawal. This is developed with close liaison with the English department and will involve students from years 1 to 5. These students will also be supported within the classroom.

Continue developing Cross/Curricular Skills in Personal and Social Education by means of classroom support and in-service training.

Statemented Students will have an additional hours tutor.

With close liaison with E.W.O., School Psychologist, Heads of House, Form Tutors, Staff involved and Parents we will devise programmes to encourage access back into the curriculum, for students with attendance problems.

As well as flexible withdrawal groups for literacy with emphasis on the lower school in particular, to give them a good start in the first two years, there will be a continuation of support in the classroom for each first year form and some second years. Limited support for other years.

Clinic sessions on a self referral and staff referral basis will continue.

There will also be a continuation of Cross/Age tutoring in reading three dinner times a week.

Continuation of reading at home by the regular borrowing of books and encouragement of parental involvement.

Advice on reading methods given to parents by means of home contact and visits.

As well as visits to the home parents will be encouraged to attend informal meetings at the Curriculum Support Base.

Support of S.N. students who are involved in residential activities.

1992/93

We will review progress made in previous year.

Review of schemes of work and resources provided in Science and English.

National Curriculum has started in Maths and Humanities and will be targeted to develop differentiated teaching resources and methods in both subject areas.

There will be close contact with the Maths and Humanities advisers and S.E.N. area co-ordinator.

Continue Cross/Age tutoring and parental involvement in reading at home.

Continue Support of S.N. students who are involved in residential activities.

Continuation of flexible withdrawal and support of students with learning difficulties and ensure provision of tutors for statemented students.

Continued links with E.W.O., School Psychologist, Heads of House, Form Tutors, Parents and any other relevant outside agencies to help to continue programmes to encourage access back into the curriculum for students with attendance problems.

Review recording and assessment system and adjust where necessary.

Continue staff/self referral of students and improve where necessary.

Continuation and review of staff inset.

Development of Maths and Humanities areas in Curriculum Support Base and continue to develop links with I.T. and library area.

Curriculum Support Base meetings will be arranged with the Maths department in the autumn term by which time the Maths area will be started.

Feedback onn progress made in Maths by the end of the autumn term including open day of curriculum support base with sharing of ideas.

D

Curriculum Support Base meetings will be arranged with the Humanities department in the summer term by which time the Humanities area will be started.

Feedback on progress made in Humanities by the end of the summer term including Open Day of Curriculum Support Base with sharing of ideas.

Further strengthening of links and consultations with departments.

Continuation of positive input into Head of Department and department meetings.

Continuation of links with the Special Needs Careers Officer and post 16 Special Needs Advisory Service and Rathbone Society.

Review of recording and assessment system and adjust where necessary.

1993/94

Review of previous years and continuation of policies which have proved a success.

Liaise with Design/Technology and History departments with reference to the National Curriculum and review links with other departments that have already been established.

Close contact with the Design/Technology adviser, History adviser and S.E.N. area co-ordinator.

Development of Design/Technology and History areas in Curriculum Support Base and continue to develop links with I.T. and Library area.

Curriculum Support Base meetings will be arranged with the Design/ Technology departments in the autumn term by which time the Design/ Technology area will be started.

Feedback on progress made in Design/Technology by the end of the autumn term including Open Day of Curriculum Support base with sharing of ideas.

Curriculum Support Base meetings will be arranged with the History department in the summer term by which time the History area will be started.

Feedback on progress made in History by the end of the summer term including Open Day of Curriculum Support Base with sharing of ideas.

The Curriculum Support Department to continue to be a catalyst for the development of a whole school approach. Staff working together developing resources to facilitate differentiated learning.

Several features can be highlighted in these extracts from New Parks Community College's development plan.

- Page 78 sets the context for the five year plan.
- Pages 79 to 85 give an outline of priorities under six main headings.
- Pages 86 to 90 take an element — curriculum support — and show the detailed developments which have been planned for a two year period and which are reflected in the overall plan for the school.

This represents a good example of a school that is developing its planning approach and, together with other specific material which has not been included here, makes it a comprehensive and very usable document with many excellent features. The use of information in a schematic form on pages 84 and 85 is a useful approach which has been developed in a number of schools.

We have worked on school development plans with a group of Bexley headteachers who, among other things, give a brief prose résumé and then focus on the approach outlined in Section Four of our report format (*see* page 19), providing a schematic representation for action plans. This is a very good example of trying to represent the overall pattern of action points in a school development plan in a strategic way to enable the user to have a clear overview of the critical decision areas. In Figures 5.3 to 5.10 we replicate their draft work for a primary and a secondary school (including, in each case, a detailed plan for one of the subunits) as an indicator of this type of approach.

Brentwich Primary School — Whole School Development Plan 1991–92

The school has continued to develop its curriculum policies and the whole staff have been involved in discussion, consultations and decision-making meetings. Governors will appreciate that much of this work has to be carried out either after the working day or at home with the preparation of documents and plans. All staff have this commitment.

The two new members of the staff have quickly complemented the present work of the school and each has expertise which will be developed next year, in particular drama and music.

The policy of parental involvement has been enhanced by a review of the Parents' Evening to involve discussion based on a written document available prior to the interview. The production of a booklet on reading and maths, and a home school contact book has met with favourable comments from a number of parents. A series of open days is planned for next year.

Curriculum development will focus on three areas. First, a review of present practice will be undertaken. It is recognised that the maths scheme does not deliver the National Curriculum and will need to be replaced. A survey of new schemes will be undertaken. It is anticipated that £3,500 will be required to purchase new materials. Sponsorship will be sought from local/national industry.

Secondly, a home reading policy is to be launched. This will require additional books to be purchased to ensure sufficient high quality literature to be available. The PTA is to be approached to provide funds and £1,000 should be allocated from school capitation. It is planned to launch the project with an evening meeting with an outside speaker for parents in October.

Thirdly, in order to fulfil legal requirements of the national curriculum, a teaching programme for the delivery of history and geography must be formulated. Task groups will be formed, led by the curriculum leaders and will work throughout the Spring term to produce draft guidelines and policies. The inspectors' report indicated a lack of resources in these areas and an audit undertaken recently has supported this observation. Funding for new resources must be provided. A sum of £750 will partially offset these deficiencies.

In order to address the problem of providing non-contact time for curriculum consultants it is planned to appoint two part-time (1 full-time equivalent) teachers to support KS1 and KS2 staff each morning. 12.0 Staff will be class-based and our present 0.6 teacher will continue to support pupils with reading problems. Training in IT must be provided for her to enable the computer assisted reading programme to be used effectively. A bid for 14 days advisory teacher support has been accepted by the LEA. Advisory teachers will support classroom teachers in humanities (6 days), problem solving in mathematics (6 days), and art (2 days).

The staff of the school are aware that the present arrangements for reporting pupil progress to parents and explaining school policies to them are limited and need improving. This is a major area of concern. It is planned, as a first stage, to improve the arrangements for the organisation and conduct of open evenings. A working party of teachers with a parent from the governing body will be charged to produce an initial report by November. The arrangements for lunch time are causing problems. An increasing number of pupils bring sandwiches and few activities are provided for them over this hour and a quarter period. Discipline becomes a problem and children are patently bored. We need to review our arrangements and look to other schools for possible improvements. The involvement of lunchtime supervisors/ancillaries will need to be secured in bringing about change.

In the light of the National Conditions of Service and in line with the introduction of appraisal procedures it will be necessary, during the year, to review posts of special responsibility and reallocate them to reflect the curriculum and management requirements of the school. Job descriptions need to be agreed with all staff (teaching and non-teaching) and this will require the equivalent of three days supply cover to allow staff release.

The advent of LMS in April 1993 will mean the absence of the head, deputy and secretary in specific training. Governors will also receive training in this major development. The school will need to carry out a resource audit and a budgetary review. This is seen as a high priority. Other forms of gaining finance will need to be explored and sponsorship needs to be examined, particularly for a new maths scheme which is urgently needed to meet national curriculum requirements.

It is essential that the school roll is maintained, or improved. The optimum number appears to be between 390 and 400 pupils and efforts need to be made to achieve this over a three year period. Positive marketing needs to be in place.

The school is to be inspected in October and the recommendations will be set alongside our own school review which we intend to carry out during September.

Record keeping continues to develop and be modified in the light of initiatives from the national curriculum, which can be absorbed into the present format of professional judgement, testing, and individual pupil records. Each pupil also has a portfolio of work which follows him/her throughout the seven years at school.

The school has cooperated with two local polytechnics and has received students both on an observation basis and for full teaching practice. Staff have been willing to give time to this.

Figure 5.3: Brentwich Primary School — whole school development plan 1991–92 — (summary statement)

Figure 5.4   **SCHOOL MANAGEMENT DEVELOPMENT PLAN:**

WHOLE SCHOOL PLAN	YEAR 1 (1991–92)	YEAR 2 (1992–93)
CURRICULUM and CURRICULUM DEVELOPMENT	FOCUS 1. Maths 2. Launch home reading policy 3. History/geography guidelines	1. Continue Year 1 2. Art 3. Music
PUPIL WELFARE PASTORAL CARE	1. Maintain and improve open evening structures 2. Re-organise lunchtime arrangements	1. Provide entry profile for pupils/parents 2. Establish 'New Parents' meetings and pupil induction scheme
HUMAN RESOURCES	1. Extend ancillary help 2. Curriculum (from above) — non-contract time 12 days 3. Advisory Service 14 days 4. 13.6 + HT required (2 new staff) to be recruited and inducted Involvement of lunchtime and other staff in school	1. Increased parental help within school 2. Retirement of deputy head
MANAGEMENT STRUCTURES and APPROACHES	1. Review PSRs and re-allocate Construct job descriptions 2. Involve all staff in school development plan	1. LMS delegation 2. Establish working groups with governing body 3. Establish appraisal system
PHYSICAL and FINANCIAL RESOURCES	1. Undertake budgetary review 2. Undertake resource audit 3. Examine use of non-teaching space 4. Seek sponsorship for maths scheme 5. Examine expenditure under formula funding	1. Set up ecology/learning area in grounds
PUPIL ROLL and MARKETING	Estimated roll at September 368 1. Re-write information for Parents	Estimated roll 391 1. New school uniform 2. School production at Easter
MONITORING and EVALUATION MECHANISMS	1. Establish school self-review system (GRIDS)	1. Assessment Policy 2. Parental Questionnaire
NATIONAL/LOCAL INITIATIVES	1. NC Records 2. History/Geography	Art/Music
OTHERS	Students to be allocated and supervised	1. Art Week/Artist in residence 2. Art Course to be held in school

BRENTWICH PRIMARY SCHOOL

| YEAR 3 (1993-94) | YEAR 1 (1991–92) | |
	TIME TARGETS (including cycle of governors' meetings)	SUCCESS CRITERIA Performance indicators
1. Continue Year 2 2. PE 3. Assessment KS 2	1. Summer 2. Autumn 3. Spring	
1. Review and rewrite behaviour policy 2. Consider holiday plan scheme	1. Spring 2. Autumn	
1. Launch Parents' Association 2. Appoint part-time Bursar on shared basis	1. Spring 2. INSET needs to LEA by October 1991 3. Application for LEA courses and advisory support January 1992	
1. Staff Handbook to produce	1. Autumn	
1. Review all contracts 2. Governors to request additional storage resources from LEA	1. Spring 2. Autumn 3. Summer 4. Ongoing 5. Ongoing	
Estimated roll 393 1. Develop close links with playgroups	Form 7 for DES/LEA Jan 1992 1. Summer	
KS 2 Assessment		

Brentwich Primary School — Maths Developments 1991–92

It has been possible to complete a review of the maths work within the school which has harmonised the approach throughout the complete age range. I am grateful to my colleagues for the comments during staff meetings and through individual contacts and working groups. Since I have had to take time from my class work — non-contact time — to coordinate the work, this has meant that the daily timetables have been disrupted.

Certain elements have emerged and been highlighted by the series of meetings arranged during the year. It has been possible to address the following:

1. Record keeping has been agreed and will be implemented next year.
2. More equipment to augment practical apparatus for Years 1–3 has been acquired. Deficiencies in provision for Years 3–4 need to be looked at next year.
3. Work has been done by Year 2 teachers but SATS have meant this was limited.
4. The storage areas have been established and now represent a central resource — there will need to be a financial commitment to this next term.
5. Although a parents' evening was arranged this was not held because of illness and staffing problems. The launch of the new scheme is expected next term.

Figure 5.5: Subunit plan — primary mathematics — (summary statement)

Subunit plan —

primary mathematics —

(schematic diagram)

Figure   5.6

Figure 5.6   **SCHOOL MANAGEMENT DEVELOPMENT PLAN:**

AREA OF ACTIVITY Mathematics (Curriculum Area/Head of year)	YEAR 1 (1991–92)	YEAR 2 (1992–93)
CURRICULUM including RoA developments Assessments	1. Review of school's Maths policy document 2. Review SATS and NC record keeping and develop improved scheme	1. Reviewed policy in place 2. Develop record keeping policy 3. Assess needs for special needs in Maths
ORGANISATION	1. Staff meetings for above 2. Working parties to review record keeping 3. Visits to other schools/classes	1. Target support teachers on Maths 2. Computer support for slow learners 3. Meetings for parents on new scheme
HUMAN RESOURCES	1. New contact for curriculum involvement of parents 2. Advisory Service — 4 days AT time 3. Ancillary/parents group to work in KS2	1. INSET for whole staff 2. 1 'Baker Day' + Advisory Teacher support
FINANCIAL RESOURCES	1. Production of policy document 2. Purchase of equipment £1,000 3. Cost of non-contact time £300 4. Replacement/renewal of maths scheme £2,000	1. Replacement/renewal Maths scheme £1,000 2. Purchase of equipment £500 3. Explore external funding
PHYSICAL RESOURCES	1. Create new storage space areas 2. Form central resource for maths equipment	
QUALITY ASSURANCE (quality delivery to pupils)	1. Evaluate Maths schemes for KS1 and KS2	1. Post holder to evaluate learning in pupils and report to staff/governors

BRENTWICH PRIMARY SCHOOL

YEAR 3 (1993-94)	YEAR 1 (1991–92)		
	TIME TARGETS	SUCCESS CRITERIA Performance indicators	
1. Review record keeping policy 2. KS 2 Maths — prepare for end of Key Stage assessment 3. Maths and cross curricular links	1. Autumn 2. Spring	
1. Staff meetings to ensure whole school approach 2. Homework policy in Maths	1. Autumn 2. Spring 3. Autumn	
1. Greater parental involvement in Maths activities	1. Spring 2. Spring/Summer 3. Summer	
1. Purchase of playground/environmental materials 2. Purchase of equipment £700	1. Autumn 2. Spring 3. Summer	
1. Review use of teaching space/storage space 2. Create learning activities 3. Using the playground and immediate environment as a teaching resource	1. Autumn 2. Spring	
1. Produce action plan from LEA inspection report	1. Spring	

Brentwich Secondary School — Whole School Development Plan 1991–92

The school has gone through a very successful year and has made considerable progress in a number of areas. Academic departments have reviewed their teaching programmes with the continued implementation of the national curriculum. Examination results have improved and the school continues to gain a significant number of higher education places. The links between parents and the school have been enhanced by the work of the PTA and the new school newsletter. Staffing has been increased during the year, with two extra appointments made and a significant programme of staff development undertaken. Pupils continue to gain success in sporting and cultural fields both within the borough and the south east region.

The governing body, working in close collaboration with the head and staff, has established key areas on which to build on past achievements to enhance provision for the future. These areas for development are summarised below.

Progress is being made towards the implementation of the national curriculum with particular reference to geography and history and monitoring the core subjects and technology. In the light of the Secretary of State's recent pronouncements in respect of education post-16, the school will need to focus particularly on the development of policy and practice in this area with the ultimate objective of raising the number of pupils staying at school after the age of 16 years.

The effective delivery of the curriculum is dependent upon a well qualified, stable and committed staff. The school has made progress in appointing staff to deliver the key tasks as identified in the plan, including the appointment of cross curricular leaders. The thrust of central government's initiative to introduce teacher appraisal will require a response from the school in terms of a plan for the implementation of an appraisal scheme which has the support of the staff as a whole. Associated with this is the process of supporting staff through INSET arrangements which form part of the school's Development Plan.

We are working with the LEA in the hope of obtaining finance for two new general purpose laboratories. We look to parents for their support of the Diamond Jubilee Appeal for a new school hall, the size of which will reflect more accurately the number of pupils in the school and which will enhance facilities for lettings.

Figure 5.7: Whole School Plan — Secondary — (summary statement)

Whole school plan —

secondary —

(schematic diagram)

Figure   5.8

Figure 5.8 **SCHOOL MANAGEMENT DEVELOPMENT PLAN:**

WHOLE SCHOOL PLAN	YEAR 1 (1991–92)	YEAR 2 (1992–93)
CURRICULUM and CURRICULUM DEVELOPMENT	1. Implement NC Geography and History 2. Monitoring NC core and technology 3. Determine 16–19 policy	1. Implement remainder of NC 2. Monitor remainder of NC and RE 3. Implementation of all cross-curricular areas 4. Review cross-curricular policies 5. Plan KS4
PUPIL WELFARE PASTORAL CARE	1. Review pastoral system 2. Develop pupil participation 3. Review SEN policy and policy for pupils at risk	1. Evaluate effectiveness of support agencies 2. Develop PSE programme 3. Implement reviewed policy
HUMAN RESOURCES	1. Appoint cross-curricular leaders 2. Appraisal training for management 3. Evaluation of support staff requirements	1. Reconsider salary structure 2. Middle management training and development 3. Implement support staff restructuring
MANAGEMENT STRUCTURES and APPROACHES	1. Write support staff job descriptions 2. Define budgeting procedures for heads of department to implement 3. Establish constitution for governing body and committees	1. Review teachers' job descriptions 2. Introduce budgeting procedures and monitor 3. Implement new structure
PHYSICAL and FINANCIAL RESOURCES	1. Obtain finance for two laboratories 2. Launch appeal for school hall 3. Extend networking to senior management	1. Build laboratories 2. Continue appeal 3. Extend networking to heads of year
PUPIL ROLL and MARKETING	Estimated roll 870 1. Write prospectus 2. Develop contact with out-LEA primary schools ————▶ 3. Maintain numbers in sixth form ————▶	Estimated roll 880 1. Refine marketing targets
MONITORING and EVALUATION MECHANISMS	1. Review 11–16 policy 2. Exam results evaluation 3. Monitor and evaluate homework policy ————▶	1. Monitor implementation of job descriptions 2. Monitor assesment policy 3. Review homework policy
PARENTS and COMMUNITY	1. Extend information about curriculum 2. Establish industry links	1. Obtain parental evaluation of curriculum information 2. Monitor and review industry links 3. Review format of annual governor/parent meeting

BRENTWICH SECONDARY SCHOOL

YEAR 3 (1993-94)	YEAR 1 (1991–92)	
	TIME TARGETS (including cycle of governors' meetings)	SUCCESS CRITERIA Performance indicators
1. Implement SATS for History and Geography 2. Develop vocational qualifications and courses 3. Review post-16 curriculum	1. Implement September 1991 2. July 1992 3. January 1992	
1. Develop contractual arrangements with support agencies 2. Review equal opportunities policy 3. Abandon school uniform	Working parties to report: 1. December 1991 2. April 1992 3. December 1992	
1. Staff training re: networking 2. Establish personnel approach for staff management 3. Appoint new headteacher	INSET needs to LEA by October 1991 Application for LEA courses and advisory help by Jan 1992 1. September 1991 2. To be completed by April 1992 3. April 1992	
1. Reassess senior management roles 2. Review, evaluate and revise procedures 3. Appoint bursar on retirement of DHT	1. July 1992 2. January 1992 3. September 1991	
1. Equip laboratories 2. Build hall 3. Accommodation for bursar 4. Adequate network for entire school/training	1. Detailed bid to LEA by June 1991 2. September 1991 3. July 1992	
1. Estimated roll 900 → →	Form 7 for DES/LEA by Jan 1992 1. January 1992 2. January–April 1992 3. September 1992	
→ Monitor open enrolment policy	1. April 1992 2. September 1991 3. April 1992	
1. Invite Secretary of State to open hall and laboratories 2. Investigate community use of school	1. November 1991 2. April 1992	

Brentwich Secondary School — History Department Plan 1991–92

During the year, staffing in the department has been enhanced by the appointment of Mrs Jones which has led to a reallocation of classes and duties within the department. National curriculum implementation and the associated training has continued with Years 7, 8 and 9. A key need for the next year is the development of schemes of work for national curriculum KS3 linked to the levels of study identified in statutory orders. This will be undertaken by a departmental working party led by Mr Smith following his recent promotion. The reintroduction of field work is considered a priority this year, although the school's charging policy will need to be considered. These field studies in Year 9 will respond to the Government's emphasis on environmental issues.

Staff development will need to focus on skills in information technology to develop simulation exercises and to assist in assessment. Relevant computer hardware and appropriate software have been identified and the departmental bid to the finance committee will reflect these needs. The security system will need to be upgraded.

The Head of Department is receiving appraisal training with a view to monitoring more effectively the work of the department. During the year performance indicators for assessing development and success will be agreed.

Figure 5.9: Subunit plan — Secondary history — (summary statement)

Subunit plan —

secondary history —

(schematic diagram)

Figure   5.10

Figure 5.10   **SCHOOL MANAGEMENT DEVELOPMENT PLAN:**

AREA OF ACTIVITY: History Department (Curriculum Area/Head of year)	YEAR 1 (1991–92)	YEAR 2 (1992–93)
CURRICULUM including RoA developments Assessment	1. Introduction of NC Year 7 (KS 3) 2. Prepare syllabus and assessment for Year 8 3. Seek to reintroduce field work in Year 9	1. Continuing NC into Year 8 2. Prepare syllabus and assessment for Year 9, including SATS 3. Look at other A-level schemes
ORGANISATION	1. Departmental Working Party to determine scheme of work/ assessment 2. Review work/structure of departmental meetings 3. Review staff responsibilities in the department	1. Review and modify schemes developed in 1991–92 2. Link assessment to RoA criteria
HUMAN RESOURCES	1. Training of staff to teach Units for Year 8 2. Appraisal training for Head of Department 3. IT skill development for department staff	1. Appraisal training for members of department
FINANCIAL RESOURCES	1. Identify computer hardware and software requirements 2. Extra resources for options in Years 10 and 11 3. Core texts for Year 8	1. Commitment for financial support for local study/field work 2. Increase NC expenditure following evaluation of materials 3. Core texts for Year 9
PHYSICAL RESOURCES	1. Increase storage facilities and shelving 2. Change blackboard for white board 3. Extend security system	Permanent base for lower school history
QUALITY ASSURANCE (quality delivery to students/pupils)	1. Programme observation of department staff teaching 2. Establish criteria for assessing development and success	Evaluate effectiveness of computer training

BRENTWICH SECONDARY SCHOOL

YEAR 3 (1993-94)	YEAR 1 (1991–92)		
	TIME TARGETS		SUCCESS CRITERIA
1. Preparation for KS 4 years 10 and 11 2. Consolidate years 7 and 8	Autumn Spring Summer	Core study Unit 1 Roman Empire Core Study Unit 2 Med Britain Supplementary Unit Reformation and Counter Reformation	
	Autumn Spring	Review staff responsibilities Curriculum planning	
Consideration of department's ability to recruit students for KS 4	Autumn Spring Summer	Appraisal training IT skills training Staff training for Year 8 units	
Increase NC expenditure following evaluation of materials for KS 4	Autumn Spring Summer	Computer *in situ* to accommodate RoA and other requirements Resources for Years 10 and 11 Texts for Year 8	
Redecoration of history teaching areas	Autumn Spring Summer	Increase storage Extended security Change boards	
Review KS 3 planning and assessment	Autumn Spring	Criteria for assessing development and success Observation of department teaching	

We believe that the Bexley approach has a great deal to commend it. There is a very significant use for the time targets and success criteria which are put in the final column. These should form the basis of negotiation between the headteacher and the member of staff responsible for the curriculum area as a means of planning, setting targets, sequencing activities and evaluating the success in achieving the targets set. This framework can provide a powerful motivating device if joint agreement and consensus is reached, rather than just having a set of arbitrarily imposed targets. Similarly, the extent to which the whole school time targets and success criteria have been achieved can be one of the means of appraising the senior management team. In the Bexley examples this negotiation process had not been completed at this draft stage so that, in the plans shown as Figures 5.4 to 5.10, the final columns remain blank.

Drawing these threads together, we can consider what would be the important content features of a good report. In Chapter Two we outlined the following strategic elements which we felt should be stated and communicated to the partners as a whole school development plan document.

Section One: A profile of the school, including its aims

Section Two: A summary of trends (internal and external)

Section Three: A central plan giving medium term developments

Section Four: An action plan for the coming year to include:

       • short term objectives

       • targets, tasks, timing and indicators of success

       • resource implications

Figure 5.11:   Components of a whole school development plan

We now develop these categories in order to give guidance to those creating this whole school plan.

Section One: A profile of the school, including its aims

This is the first contextual statement. Although it would be reexamined annually, it would not normally be subject to major change from year to year. Such a statement would include:

- The type of school;
- The community and environment in which the school operates;
- The mission statement of school;
- The aims of school;
- Outlines of pupil and staff organisation; and
- Key factors related to teaching and learning.

Section Two: A summary of trends (internal and external)

This section would form a more dynamic contextual statement to reflect the major changes which are occurring in education both locally and nationally and, perhaps, the changes in the local community. Amongst many factors, it could include aspects of the following:

- The national curriculum;
- Central government policy developments concerning teaching and learning;
- Appraisal;
- Powers and responsibilities under LMS or GM status;
- Open enrolment;
- Staffing availability;
- The national and local economy;
- Local housing; and
- Local demography.

Section Three: A central plan giving medium-term developments

---

Before detailed planning can take place, the school needs to establish the broad development themes that it will follow over the medium term. This will allow immediate action plans to be set within a three year context. This section would be a descriptive account of the proposed activities needed to take the school forward to its goals and aims. It will describe the main developments which are to take place within the school and will show the links between the different elements. For example, if there needs to be a major revision of the way that the school teaches information technology, the whole school plan will highlight the need for curriculum planning, equipment and materials, staff development and physical resources for example the associated electrical systems.

In addition to the plans for the coming year, this section will outline the future implications of the coming year's projects and will point to the developments which will be required over the next two years.

Section Four: An action plan for the coming year

This plan would include:

- Short-term objectives;
- Targets, tasks, timing and indicators of success; and
- Resource implications.

We suggest that, in this section, the various elements of the school development plan are summarised by placing them as the rows in a matrix and setting them against columns which summarise the objectives, tasks and performance indicators. Figures 5.12 and 5.13 show the blank matrix for the whole school and for a curricular subunit. Schools could use these in order to devise the most appropriate format for the core and support elements.

Matrix for a

whole school

development plan

Figure   5.12

Figure 5.12   **SCHOOL MANAGEMENT DEVELOPMENT PLAN:**

WHOLE SCHOOL PLAN	YEAR 1 (199 –9)	YEAR 2 (199 –9)
CURRICULUM and CURRICULUM DEVELOPMENT		
HUMAN RESOURCES		
PUPIL WELFARE PASTORAL CARE		
PHYSICAL RESOURCES		
PUPIL ROLL and MARKETING		
MANAGEMENT STRUCTURES and APPROACHES		
MONITORING and EVALUATION MECHANISMS		
FINANCIAL RESOURCES		

SCHOOL: ....

| YEAR 3 (199 -9) | YEAR 1 (199 -9) | |
	TIME TARGETS (including cycle of governors' meetings)	SUCCESS CRITERIA Performance indicators

Figure 5.13   **SCHOOL MANAGEMENT DEVELOPMENT PLAN:**

AREA OF ACTIVITY: (Curriculum Area/Head of year)	YEAR 1 (199 –9)	YEAR 2 (199 –9)
CURRICULUM including RoA developments Assesment		
ORGANISATION		
HUMAN RESOURCES		
FINANCIAL RESOURCES		
PHYSICAL RESOURCES		
QUALITY ASSURANCE		

SCHOOL: ....

YEAR 3 (199 -9)	YEAR 1 (199 -9)	
	TIME TARGETS	SUCCESS CRITERIA Performance indicators

Conclusion

This chapter has presented examples of good practice in school development planning and put forward a four part structure for a school development plan report. The way in which this can be put into practice will now be demonstrated (in Chapters Six to Nine) by providing a case study of a primary and a secondary school and then drawing up an outline school development plan for each school.

6 Primary school case study

This chapter provides the information on which to base a whole school development plan for a typical primary school. Background information is provided about the school in order to set the context. Next the work of the school is reviewed under headings which reflect the *core* and *support* elements described earlier in the book. In the following chapter the whole school development plan is constructed from this information. In a real school there would be a significantly greater volume of knowledge and information but, nevertheless, within the limits of a concise case study, we demonstrate some of the main features of the school development plan report.

Grantwich Primary School

Grantwich Primary School is a school of 287 pupils aged 5–11 years old (Group 2). The teaching staff of the school consists of the Head (who took up her post in September 1991) and 11 full-time staff equivalents.

Grantwich is a small town which has a population of 24,000. It is predominantly a dormitory town but has some light industry based on new technology. There are good road and rail links to larger industrial centres for shopping and employment. Many of the children come from a mainly middle class area with extensive private housing. About 30 per cent of the intake comes from the older part of the town from a more mixed housing stock. Most pupils comply with the school's uniform policy which recommends a maroon tee shirt and sweatshirt and grey trousers or skirt.

The school was built in the early 1950s on a traditional pattern with a hall and 11 individual classrooms. Externally there are pleasant grounds comprising two playgrounds and a large grassed area. A playgroup uses the hall on one morning a week. The school is not used for adult education and the governors' policy on lettings suggests that they have given little thought to this area of activity.

In 1983 the school adapted the list of aims which was circulated by the LEA to produce the following statement:

> The school aims to provide for the intellectual, spiritual, moral, cultural, social and physical development of its pupils.

In the immediate vicinity there are two other schools for 5–11 year olds, one a county school which moved to new buildings two years ago and the other a voluntary aided school. Both of these schools have a traditional uniform which comprises shirt, tie, blazer and trousers or skirt. There is a private preparatory school five miles away and a private nursery school in the town. With the introduction of open enrolment for primary schools, parents are increasingly looking at all schools in the town before making their choice. At the secondary stage, most of the pupils move on to Grantwich High School because the nearest alternative secondary school is over four miles away.

The new headteacher, not wishing to make any hasty decisions, has asked the staff and the school's adviser to carry out a thorough review of the school in the Autumn of 1991. This review will then form the basis of consultations and discussions before development priorities will be established. A large amount of information has been gathered and it is summarised on the following pages.

1.   Curriculum and curriculum development

The previous head saw herself as the curriculum leader. There is little whole class teaching. In general, pupils work in small groups according to their ages. It appears that little attention has been paid to differentiating the work of pupils in these groups according to ability. Part-time staff make little contribution to curriculum development: they are used for the withdrawal of pupils who are particularly poor at reading and they have also provided support during the SATs for Year 2. When necessary, they cover the first three days of teacher absence and then supply teachers are used after day three of such absence.

Mathematics

There is a maths coordinator. A new maths scheme was introduced in September 1990 for the reception class and it is gradually being extended up the school. It is ideally suited to the requirements of the national curriculum. Unfortunately, the older children are still working from very dated materials and there is a strain on teachers as they try to supplement these and make them more stimulating. Most staff have been to courses on information technology but they have not always been able to utilise the skills because each computer is shared between three or four classes. One computer is particularly old and unreliable. Strategies for recording pupil progress in mathematics seem to be working and provide useful information when the pupils move to the next class.

English

The language coordinator retired last year and has not been replaced. The reading scheme is very dated and unsuitable. The library books are not very accessible to the children and are rather dilapidated and unappealing. There are several parents who have written to the new head and offered to listen to children reading.

Science

There is a science coordinator and a scheme which meets the requirements of the national curriculum is in use throughout the school. Although there was an injection of funds when the scheme was started, little has been allocated since so that consumable materials have not been replaced quickly enough. Staff are therefore now unable to use some of the worksheets. The storage of materials needs to be improved — some larger items are not replaced after use by a particular class. Within each classroom, the storage system for small items is inadequate. Several parents work at one of the local electronics companies and have offered 'cast off' equipment and materials.

Technology

The science coordinator also looks after technology. The curriculum is being developed and materials are being built up in this area. Staff development sessions have been taking place once a month after school. Extra support in the classroom (preferably from the coordinator) is going to be needed in order to implement the changes.

History and geography

Little attention was given to these subjects until recently. A coordinator was designated and she has spent several months studying good practice in other primary schools and talking to the high school staff about their work and teaching strategies. She is almost ready to work with the staff to develop the curriculum and to plan its resourcing.

Art

Whenever the local schools are invited to send pupils' work for competitions and displays, the painting and drawing receives high praise. There is a need to develop more three-dimensional work in a range of materials. However, this has implications for the facilities provided in each classroom. Last year the school had an 'artist in residence' for a week and the pupils benefited considerably. This could be repeated at a future date, perhaps in conjunction with the development of three-dimensional work.

Music

Currently, no teacher in the school can play the piano and most class teachers feel very ill at ease in the area of music. Many of the pupils have electronic keyboards at home. The LEA's peripatetic music teacher comes to teach the recorder to the juniors who show interest (all girls) and a pupil from the high school plays the piano for assembly on Fridays. The LEA will be delegating funds for peripatetic music teaching from April 1993 and will then charge for the service on an hourly basis. It will be necessary to develop the skills of all teachers in this area and to ensure that a wider range of experiences is offered to both boys and girls. The requirements of the national curriculum will need to be incorporated into any plans.

PE and Dance

There is a coherent programme in place which develops physical skills and team building. Most of the staff feel able to deal with this area although one or two are less confident. They can arrange to exchange classes to overcome this problem. Expenditure on equipment will be needed if the school is to meet all the requirements of the national curriculum.

RE

There is a daily collective act of worship which is of a Christian nature. Pairs of classes usually get together first thing in the morning except on Fridays when the whole school meets in the hall. The coverage of RE within the curriculum is recorded meticulously by three teachers but there is no information from the others.

Cross-curricular themes

Personal, social and health education — the deputy head reports that this area has not been given any consideration by the school.

Economic and industrial understanding — again the staff have not considered this although one of the governors, who was coopted to represent local industry, has expressed concern about this omission and has offered his help.

Information technology — will never be an integral part of the pupils' work until more computers and printers are available and arrangements are made for a quick maintenance service when problems arise.

Environmental education — should be reviewed by the science coordinator — little attention has been given to this aspect of the national curriculum.

Special needs

There is no special needs coordinator or policy. Two children are statemented and share the time of a nursery nurse. Children who are weak at reading are withdrawn from their classes for ten minutes each day but otherwise receive little support or attention. There is no consideration of the needs of gifted children although parents believe that the private preparatory school caters very well for these children.

2. Human resources

Responsibility for staff development and appraisal lies with the head while a governors' staffing subcommittee deals with appointments.

When the new head took up her post in September 1991 she was informed that the previous head had been absent for several separate weeks since November 1990 when she had attended her first meeting on the full implementation of LMS. The deputy head has only been in post since September 1990 but had to assume responsibility for the school during the head's frequent absences. The previous head's management style had done little to prepare the deputy head for managing the school. It is clear that he needs development opportunities in this area if he is to

E

form part of an effective senior management team and to fulfil his ambition of gaining a headship.

In addition to the head and deputy, there are nine full-time teachers and three part-timers (0.5, 0.3, 0.2) who all have temporary one year contracts. There are no specific job descriptions and the only official coordinators are those for maths, science/technology, and history/geography. The maths coordinator has indicated her wish to take early retirement at some point within the next three years. The *ad hoc* use of the part-time teachers is giving cause for concern amongst the staff in general; the part-timers feel that they are not able to contribute to the school's development. The previous head had volunteered the school to be in the first phase of staff appraisal. The governors do not have a pay policy and have not, to date, considered offering any enhanced salaries.

There is a classroom assistant four mornings a week. She is attached to all classes which contain children of Year 2 and below. The staff recognise the value of this type of assistance and would like to see support for all classes.

There is a school secretary who should administer the budget but who feels ill at ease in this area. The clerical assistant works ten hours a week but is seeking a full-time post with more responsibility.

The caretaker is very willing to put forward suggestions for more effective maintenance and development of the school's site. The governors are keen to regrade him as a site manager and to give him greater responsibilities, including the management of energy use. Other staff and users of the school site would need to be made aware of energy efficiency issues.

Lunchtime assistants will need to be involved in the development of the positive discipline programme and have indicated that they would like to gain a wider knowledge of playground games.

For the purposes of cleaning, grounds maintenance and catering, the school is happy with the services provided through the LEA's contracting system.

Evidence from those preparing the curriculum development plan suggests the following priorities for staff development to support the curriculum:

- *English* — all staff to consider the development of a new policy and schemes of work;
- *Special Needs* (including the needs of the gifted) and cross-curricular themes — groups to review practice and needs in these areas;

- *History and Geography* — coordinator to begin to work with staff to develop policy and schemes of work; and
- *Technology* — time for coordinator to work with staff in the classroom.

3.   Pupil welfare and pastoral care

There is no one with overall responsibility for this area. Traditionally, class teachers stay with the same age range. There is an A allowance for early years (held by the teacher of the reception class) and the deputy, who teaches the oldest pupils, looks after the juniors.

The January 1992 Form 7 figures are given in Table 6.1 with the predictions for 1993.

National Curriculum Year Group	January 1992 Actual	January 1993 Predicted
6	42	41
5	41	41
4	41	37
3	37	50
2	50	33
1	33	43
R	43	37
Total	287	282

Table 6.1   Form 7 figures

As can be seen from the Form 7 figures, the number of pupils in each year group varies and it is not normally possible to have classes which comprise only one age group. Pupils are grouped chronologically so that, for example, the oldest Year 1 children are with Year 2. The ten classes are then grouped in pairs according to pupil age. The school takes rising fives in September and January so that some movements sometimes take place during the year. Although staff do not normally team teach, there are links between classes and there is some element of continuity if one teacher is absent.

The staff are not aware of any equal opportunities policy. The school is on a level site and is ideally suited for use by physically handicapped pupils. There is pressure from parents and one of the governors to make some minor conversions so that two children who currently have to travel seven miles by taxi could be accommodated at the school.

There is no formal pastoral curriculum. The school has received advice from the LEA support team and will now begin to develop a positive discipline policy.

Links with parents are limited to one parents' meeting each year when the teacher gives out the pupil's report and comments on progress. There is a lot of latent enthusiasm amongst the parents. If the school ignores this resource, it is likely that the parents will look at other schools where the parent–school partnership is stronger.

In the term preceding transfer the children visit the secondary school to which they will transfer. The deputy head is responsible for arranging this and for sending pupil records on to the secondary schools.

The school makes little call on the LEA's services such as the educational psychology service. There are very limited community links.

4. Physical resources

A team has conducted a review of the physical resources within the school. This team comprises a parent governor (who is a painter and decorator), the deputy head and the caretaker.

The five classrooms which are used by the youngest pupils were redecorated four years ago but the rest of the internal fabric was last decorated ten years ago. A rolling programme of redecoration needs to be planned. The local authority is responsible for decorating the outside of the school but it will be necessary to monitor their actions in this area otherwise the school's external appearance will have a detrimental effect on its image and on the condition of the internal fabric. The perimeter fence is the school's responsibility. The part which runs along the road requires attention soon and the painting of the whole length needs to take place within three years.

The entrance hall is quite spacious although it is cluttered by deliveries and it is difficult for visitors to alert the office staff to their presence. There is nowhere for visitors to sit. It is probable that the area could be improved by providing a table, some chairs, a noticeboard and display area.

Classroom furniture varies in style and quality. Further

discussion with teachers is required in order to plan the rationalisation, maintenance and replacement programme. This is not an immediate priority for the school.

The empty classroom is currently heated and used as a store. However, the caretaker has pointed out that there are two large storerooms which are full of very dated equipment and materials. These could be cleared so that the classroom could be put to better use. The governor thinks that the classroom should be used as an art and craft area but the deputy believes that provision of practical areas should be within or adjacent to each class. It is clear that further discussion is needed on this matter.

At the request of the Chair of Governors, an independent consultant has produced a report on energy efficiency in the school. This states that energy consumption could be reduced by expenditure on insulation and by closer control of the heating and lighting systems. It will be important to make all staff aware of this area and to allow the caretaker to have training and greater responsibility for monitoring and energy efficiency.

The curriculum review indicates the need for:

- Storage materials for science materials and equipment;
- Provision for three dimensional art;
- PE equipment and fittings; and
- Resiting of library books.

Effective staff development and record keeping would be enhanced by a resource base comprising a bookshelf and computer with printer.

5. Pupil roll and marketing

Pupil roll

It is clear that parental choice is becoming an important factor in the pupil roll but this is causing considerable unpredictability and forecasting problems. The LEA predicts that the roll will be 282 in January 1993; 275 in 1994; and 274 in 1995. These projections take account of proposed new housing on the edge of the catchment area. One of the staff knows that the other county school is considering providing minibus transport for pupils from outside its traditional catchment area. One of the governors has pointed out that, assuming funding and price increases in line with inflation, the school would experience a decrease in income of approximately £11,000 in real terms by 1995. The problem would be compounded by the incremental drift which is built into the staff salary structure. The need to increase the pupil roll is very significant although longer term enrolment figures could be increased by the relocation of central government departments to a greenfield site on the edge of the town. The empty classroom offers considerable potential for increasing the pupil roll.

Marketing

Clearly, in the competitive climate, marketing has an important place in maintaining or increasing the school roll. However, the school does not have a marketing strategy although one of the governors feels that the school should advertise the fact that it has vacancies in the local press.

The office staff point out that there is a dearth of information which can be given or sent out to people enquiring about the school. They do not feel that the current prospectus is suitable. There is also uncertainty about where to 'put' visitors who are waiting to see staff and there are no facilities to offer coffee or tea to visitors.

Staff recognise the need to enhance the school's image in the community but feel that this should take place in a planned way and that it is important to pay considerable attention to the educational product and service which is offered, rather than to an advertising campaign.

The reception teacher would like to build some links with the playgroup. Currently the parents walk in and out of school but there is no communication between the school staff and the parents.

6. Management structures and approaches

Both the existing management structure and the roles of all the partners are unclear and need thorough review and development. Amongst other things, the outcome of this process should take account of the following issues:

- The role of the governing body and its links with the staff;
- The creation of senior management team;
- The role of the head as a boundary manager;
- The management role and development of the deputy head;
- The review of allowances;
- The designation of coordinators for each curricular area;
- The need for coordinators for other purposes;
- The development of job descriptions for all staff;
- The building of teams;

- The delegation of responsibility to teams and to individuals;
- The development of the role of the administrative officer/bursar;
- The extension of the post of classroom assistant;
- The improvements in communication with parents, both for consultation and for the dissemination of information; and
- The development of wider links with the secondary school.

Clearly, these will have to be part of a long-term plan.

7.   Monitoring and evaluation mechanisms

Curriculum monitoring and pupil record keeping would be made simpler if there were a computer dedicated to staff use. There is a range of suitable software which could help with efficiency and effectiveness in this area.

Evaluation needs to be given a much higher priority so that it can inform the future development of the school. At the moment there is a lack of evidence from past activities. However, there are many changes needed over the next two or three years, and evaluation needs to be planned in conjunction with these developments, rather than as a separate activity. Consideration should be given to the range of people who will feed into the evaluation process.

The annual report to parents is produced by a subcommittee of governors but, since its inception, on average only five parents have attended the annual meeting with the governors.

8.   Financial resources

A task group has been formed to carry out the review of past and current spending and to consult other working groups on likely proposals. As the plans for the various elements unfold, the financial implications of their priorities will be built into the budgetary planning process. The task group comprises the chair of governors, the head, two other governors (a parent and an industrialist) and one of the standard scale teachers. The following factors have emerged to assist in the planning:

- The opportunity cost of the empty classroom has been discussed. It is felt that it would be unwise to make hasty decisions as to its use but that a firm decision should be made within the next year.

- It has been noted that the LMS formula income from the LEA for the 1992–93 financial year will be just over £364,000, an increase of five per cent on the previous year for the same number of pupils. Predicted inflation of six per cent in the following year would mean an income of nearly £390,000 but falling pupil numbers would reduce this by approximately £3,000.

- The PTA has not held any fund raising activities over the last five years, but there is the capacity to generate at least £1,000 a year with a potential to increase to £3,000.

- One of the governors is working with the caretaker, the secretary and two of the teachers to investigate the potential for lettings income and the way in which this might operate in a cost effective manner. Their first reports indicate the potential to generate a surplus from lettings of £200 in the first year with 25 per cent increases in each of the two subsequent years. It has been pointed out that the playgroup is not paying for its use of the school hall and that, on occasions, it is preventing the school's staff from being able to use that facility effectively. While it is an obvious marketing advantage to have parents of preschool children on the premises, a charge needs to be agreed.

- The industrialist on the governing body has reported that it is difficult to attract grants from local industry and commerce but that 'goods in kind' are readily available. This would include the opportunity of pupils to visit industrial and commercial premises and the donation to the school of computers, printers, paper and technology materials. One local company can offer a venue for staff development sessions which may be more appropriate than the use of the staffroom or school hall.

This chapter has sought to establish basic information about a primary school. The way in which it is used to form the school development plan is shown in the following chapter.

7 Grantwich Primary School — the development plan report

Having received reviews, the head of Grantwich Primary School, in consultation with the staff and governors, has prepared the whole school development plan. Initial strategic decisions have been taken and it has been decided to place less emphasis on the three elements related to pupil welfare and pastoral care; pupil roll and marketing; and monitoring and evaluation mechanisms. The head, deputy and chair of governors have written brief plans for these. In order to develop detailed plans for the other elements, teams were set up to include staff, governors and parents. Each team had to make sure that wider consultation and discussion had taken place before submitting its plan which would be similar in format to the subgroup reports as demonstrated by the Bexley approach in Chapter Five. This ensured that the needs of one element were reflected in the plans for the other elements. For example, the staff development plan would need to take account of curriculum development.

To avoid the reader being overwhelmed by this detail, we recommend that only a strategic view is presented as the overall school development plan, providing a summary of the documents that are available. It is supported by a whole series of plans in each of the separate elements.

We show in this chapter a school development plan comprising the four elements which were proposed in Chapters Two and Five.

F

Grantwich Primary School
Development plan for the academic year
1992–93

Section One: A profile of the school, including its aims

Grantwich Primary School is a school for 5–11 year olds located on the edge of a modern estate to the west of the town centre yet within easy reach of all areas of the town. Employment in the town is provided by a range of industrial and commercial companies, with the emphasis being on modern technology.

The school was built in 1952 and has solid well-maintained buildings set in pleasant grounds. The classroom are spacious and are quite well furnished. Attention is being given to enhancing the facilities in line with the development of the curriculum.

The teaching staff establishment comprises the headteacher, the deputy, nine full-time staff and three part-time staff. They are supported by a part-time classroom assistant, two office staff, a caretaker, and five lunchtime assistants. On appointment the new headteacher has initiated a full review of all activities and relationships.

Currently, the school does not have a mission statement but it is intended that this will be developed in the Summer of 1992 so that all subsequent development work has a point of reference. The existing school aims are to provide for the intellectual, spiritual, moral, cultural, social and physical development of its pupils. However, these will be rewritten after the mission statement has been agreed.

The pupils are, on the whole, eager to learn and their parents are very supportive. They are grouped in classes of approximately 26 to 30, based on age. Staff usually teach the same age range each year. Most pupils live in the school's traditional catchment area but some travel from other areas of the town. In addition, some pupils who live in the catchment area are now attending other schools. A few parents are sending their children to private schools. Taking into account these factors, the current roll of 285 is predicted by the LEA to fall marginally over the next few years, although the governors plan to enhance the school's reputation and counteract this trend.

> **Section Two:** A summary of trends (internal and external)

The phased introduction of the national curriculum continues with programmes of study for physical education being introduced from September 1992, and for art and music in September 1993. The raising of standards, particularly in literacy and numeracy, continues as a national priority and area of interest. The school has thoroughly examined its practice in these areas and this plan incorporates developments which will ensure maximum effectiveness.

Central government is continuing to make parents aware of their right to choose a school and of the success criteria by which each school might be judged. Parents are exercising their rights under open enrolment legislation and the school must develop a quality product and an effective marketing strategy if it is to retain pupils. There are plans for new housing on the edge of the catchment area but existing new developments are only selling very slowly so it is unlikely that there will be a noticeable effect on the pupil roll in the near future. The relocation of central government departments will definitely take place from 1993–95. However, this will not necessarily affect the number of children living in Grantwich.

Government and media emphasis has meant an increased focus on test scores. Although the school has addressed this issue, it is determined not to neglect other aspects of a child's education and development. There are national pressures to adopt certain teaching styles but the school needs to review this area before making changes. There are no higher education institutions in the area so changes in the focus of teacher training will have little effect in the near future.

The school has fully delegated powers under LMS so it is important to share responsibilities in order to prevent centralised decision-making from ignoring key contributors. There will be implications here for roles and responsibilities and a need for training for all staff. The LEA continues to delegate more spending categories to schools. While this gives more funds and wider choice to schools, it requires more careful planning. There is also the danger that some LEA services, if not used in the early stages, will become non-viable and will therefore close, thus reducing choice in the future.

Nationally and locally there are pressures to hold down public spending so that the school's budget does not expand in line with pay and price rises. This means that it is very difficult to improve the quality and quantity of resources. Locally, unemployment is rising and is currently eight per cent. This affects the income level of parents, increasing family stress which impacts on their children.

All staff in the school will be involved in the appraisal process from September 1992 but it will take about three years to fully implement and develop the process. When teaching posts are advertised there is usually a good field of experienced applicants.

Section Three: A central plan giving medium-term developments

---

The school's medium-term development plans focus round a number of themes:

- Moving ahead with national curriculum developments in a number of areas, specifically English, history, geography, music, art and cross-curricular themes;

- Clarification of roles and responsibilities in the school and the development of staff to fulfil these effectively. This needs to be built on a framework of staff development and appraisal which the school is establishing;

- Relationships between the school and its clients will be constantly reviewed over the next few years. Major work will focus on improving home–school links, parental involvement in school and the revitalisation of the PTA. This work needs to be set alongside the marketing policy and plan for the school;

- Quality of the physical environment is to be further improved over the next three years and a rolling programme of refurbishment and redecoration will ensure continuing high standards in this area.

- Improving the quality of the educational process and

its outcomes will assume an obvious high priority. This will need to be operationalised through review of monitoring and evaluation mechanisms within the school. As a self-managing school within a delegated financial framework the school will have to take on board more systematic self-evaluation procedures and evaluate the impact of the new inspection procedures;

- Success of these initiatives is obviously dependent on the financial health of the school. The current balanced budget position will need to be carefully monitored and other potential areas of income explored over the next three years if adequate resources are to be secured to implement effective education. It is hoped that a successful marketing policy will be developed and implemented and, with stronger parental links, the pupil roll should rise, giving financial benefits in terms of pupil-led funding and economies of scale.

Section Four: An action plan for the coming year

Each of the individual curricular areas and the curricular and other elements in the development plan have produced their own action plans. They are available for detailed inspection on request at the school. What follows is the aggregation of this data with other information to form the whole school Action Plan. It focuses on 1992–93 in terms of detail, time targets and success criteria but it is set within a medium-term context. For practical use this whole school plan is presented in Figure 7.1 in schematic form in order to focus management decision-making.

Figure 7.1   **SCHOOL MANAGEMENT DEVELOPMENT PLAN:**

WHOLE SCHOOL PLAN	YEAR 1 (1992–93)	YEAR 2 (1993–94)
CURRICULUM and CURRICULUM DEVELOPMENT	1. Extend maths scheme to Y2 and Y3 → Y4 and Y5— 2. Develop and implement language policy → Parental involvement → 3. Develop history and geography policies 4. Review cross-curricular themes	3. Implement history and geography policies 4. Implement cross-curricular themes
HUMAN RESOURCES	1. Review job descriptions (all staff) 2. Free time for technology coordinator 3. Implement appraisal scheme	1. Designate new roles and responsibilities 2. Develop pay policy 3. Continue appraisal process
PUPIL WELFARE PASTORAL CARE	1. Special needs/gifted provision reviewed 2. Review reporting to parents 3. Develop positive discipline policy	1. Establish equal opportunities policy 2. Improve secondary school links 3. Implement new discipline policy
PHYSICAL RESOURCES	1. Refurbish entrance hall 2. Discuss use of empty classroom 3. Reorganise storage facilities 4. Implement energy efficiency measures	1. Start rolling programme of redecoration 2. Paint perimeter fence 3. Designate site manager 4. Classroom minor works — art
PUPIL ROLL and MARKETING	Estimated roll: [282] 1. Marketing group established 2. Enhanced parental links 3. Prospectus (revise)	Estimated roll [275 + 10?] 1. Operationalise marketing plan 2. Review school uniform
MANAGEMENT STRUCTURES and APPROACHES	1. Review management roles 2. Improve internal and external communications 3. More management time for meetings	1. Develop and build management teams 2. Review progress in communications
MONITORING and EVALUATION MECHANISMS	1. Review existing evaluation approaches 2. Check reporting mechanisms to parents 3. Pupil records on computer	1. Undertake GRIDS exercise 2. Review governors role 3. Develop teacher skills in self-evaluation
FINANCIAL RESOURCES	1. Review potential income from all sources 2. Collate expenditure plans from other details 3. Monitor monthly outcomes 4. Complete transfer of manual documents to SIMS system	1. Produce PTA fundraising plans 2. Evaluate sponsorship opportunities 3. Review use of SIMS financial system

GRANTWICH PRIMARY SCHOOL

YEAR 3 (1994-95)	YEAR 1 (1992–93)	
	TIME TARGETS (including cycle of governors' meetings)	SUCCESS CRITERIA Performance indicators
──────────────▶Y6 Reading scheme──────▶Library──▶ 3. Monitor and evaluate history and geography 4. Monitor and evaluate cross curricular themes	1. Autumn 2. All year 3. Spring 4. Summer	1. In use with Y2 and Y3 2. Language policy approved by governors 3. Schemes of work 4. Schemes of work
1. Appoint music teacher 2. Implement pay policy 3. Evaluate appraisal scheme	1. By end of summer 2. Autumn 3. Spring	1. Descriptions written and published 2. Time off timetable 3. All staff appraised by Easter
1. Implement equal opportunities policy 2. Review home/school links 3. Evaluate discipline policy	1. Spring 2. Summer 3. Autumn	1. Policy document 2. New schedule 3. Policy and plan approved
1. Start rolling programme of furniture replacement Classroom minor works — art	1. By April 2. Spring 3. Autumn 4. Summer	1. Refurbishment completed 2. List of possible uses 3. Effective storage 4. Lower energy use
Estimated roll: 276 + 16? 1. Establish quality measures for communication to parents	1. All year 2. Summer 3. Spring	1. Marketing plan 2. Improved links 3. New prospectus
1. Delegate responsibilities to teams	1. Spring 2. Summer 3. Immediate	1. New descriptions 2. Staff and parent survey results 3. Designated time off
1. Implement new procedures 2. Joint governors/staff procedures	1. All year 2. Spring 3. Summer	1. Report produced 2. Parent survey 3. Records on computer
1. Review financial operating procedures 2. Review decision-making groups	1. All year 2. Autumn 3. All year 4. By April	1. Spreadsheet produced 2. Summary report 3. Discussions taken place 4. Computer system operable

8 Secondary school case study

This chapter provides the information from which to build up a whole school development plan for a typical secondary school. Background information is provided about the school in order to set the context. Next the work of the school is reviewed under side headings which reflect the *core* and *support* elements which were described in Chapter Three. The whole school development plan is created in Chapter Nine.

Grantwich High School

The high school is a mixed comprehensive school of 816 pupils (Group 5) aged 11 to 18 years old at January 1992. It was formed in 1978 when a grammar school was reorganised to become a comprehensive school. The school is on a single site in buildings which were opened in 1933 and renovated and extended in 1977.

Grantwich is a small town which has a population of 24,000. It is predominantly a dormitory town but has some light industry based on new technology. There are good road and rail links to larger industrial centres for shopping and employment. Most pupils come from middle class areas with extensive private housing. Approximately 20 per cent of the intake comes from the industrial part of the town from a more mixed housing stock. The school also draws pupils from the surrounding villages which are set in good farming territory. The school takes pupils into Year 7 from four main feeder primary schools with small numbers coming from about five other schools. The tendency to attract some pupils from outside the traditional catchment area has been a noticeable feature in the last year or two. The nearest secondary school is over four miles away and the FE College is some 6 miles away.

The school has a uniform policy which states that pupils below the sixth form will wear navy blue jumper, grey skirt/trousers, white blouse/shirt, black/blue shoes and a school tie.

There are links with the community through music, drama, business studies and work experience but these links could be expanded and developed. There is no adult education use of the building. The governors' policy on lettings indicates their lack of awareness or interest in this area.

The school aims are defined as follows:

> The school aims to provide a caring environment which offers a broad and balanced curriculum. This will prepare pupils for the opportunities, responsibilities and experiences of life in a rapidly changing world. Great emphasis is placed on developing the abilities and talents of each pupil.

1.   Curriculum and curriculum development

The deputy head (academic) works with the heads of departments to manage this element. The timetable is divided into 40 x 35 minute periods per week.

Pupils join the school at 11 + (Year 7) and, for the first three years they study the national curriculum subjects plus drama. In addition to the core and foundation subjects, all pupils should cover the cross-curricular themes such as economic and industrial understanding and information technology. Many pupils study an additional foreign language from Year 8, although this means that they have less time in creative arts and PE. In Years 10 and 11 pupils continue to follow courses in the core and foundation subjects. All of these subjects are offered at GCSE and, in addition, pupils may take three optional courses from art, business studies, French and business studies, CDT communication, CDT realisation, CDT technology, drama and home economics. The selection of courses for study in Years 10 and 11 is made during Year 9.

Mathematics

This area of the curriculum was recently the subject of an external inspection. The report was very complimentary about the schemes of work and the teaching materials available. However, some members of staff are not following the schemes, particularly in relation to more practical topics. The centralisation of most of the school's computers does not allow pupils to use these appropriately. The second in department has indicated her desire to gain more knowledge of management in education. Most of the departmental staff feel that they would be prepared to teach one more period a week if there could be a technician to look after the teaching materials and equipment.

English and drama

The head of department has been in post for a year and has reviewed the schemes of work and the strengths of the staff. It is clear that some staff find the organisation of speaking and listening aspects difficult to manage so that they need help with planning in this area. An audit of books shows that many copies go astray, probably through careless stock keeping rather than deliberate theft.

The school librarian is to retire soon and it is unclear whether she will be replaced. There are indications that the governors feel that a member of the English department could do the job for an A allowance. An older member of staff has pointed out that the school used to have a regular injection of cash for library books from the Hodgkin Trust Fund which was set up in the nineteenth century to benefit young people.

The centralisation of the school's computers means that wordprocessing can only be used in a planned way if a teacher books a room and takes the whole class. There is a need to set up a resource base within the English department or, better still, to have IT facilities in every classroom.

Modern languages

All pupils study at least one foreign language to the end of Year 11. In Years 10 and 11 this may be in combination with business studies. There is some dissatisfaction amongst parents that German is limited to the pupils who show the greatest aptitude for French at the end of Year 8. All the department's staff are agreed that this is the correct policy, despite the fact that several other schools in the region are offering German and Spanish to pupils of any ability. The staff would like the school to purchase a large house near Grantwich's twin town in France. This would provide an ideal base for language visits and also for school holidays of a more general nature. It could be let out to other educational institutions in order to increase its viability.

Science

The school has taught integrated science for many years and most parents are happy with the quality of the work. The staff share the development of units of work and all written material is stored in filing cabinets. There are problems with keeping the files in order and with replacing stock as levels fall. The technicians are under a lot of pressure because of the wide range of materials which needs to be available. The head of department feels that some of the more recently appointed staff are not really committed to the integrated approach and are focusing too much attention on their favoured disciplines. They are also unwilling to spend time developing their knowledge of the other disciplines. This is particularly the case with the staff who have come from industry.

Now that formal test results are available for each child, the department must demonstrate that it is using this information to remedy individual pupils' weaknesses and also that general departmental problems are being tackled.

Design and technology

In Years 7, 8 and 9 the technology course is an integrated one which is taught by staff with CDT, home economics, art, IT and business studies expertise. This has required considerable changes in attitudes to curricular boundaries and has meant that staff have had to plan with people whom they consider have very different backgrounds and interests. The head of CDT was given overall responsibility for this area but he was unhappy with the new approach and has recently left to start his own business. The head of home economics is now the coordinator. She feels that the boundaries will only be broken down if all the staff who teach in this area spend at least two days in a residential environment with some outside assistance such as an adviser. This is planned to take place in the very near future.

There will then be a need to revisit the overambitious projects that have been designed so far and to provide more realistic challenges for the pupils. The siting of equipment needs to be reconsidered because at the moment too many pupils are wandering around looking for equipment, materials and assistance.

Business studies

As well as being involved in the preparation and delivery of Technology in Years 7, 8 and 9, the staff of the business studies department also offer GCSE business studies as an option and teach part of the syllabus for French and business studies with the help and guidance of the modern languages department. Sixth form provision is limited to secretarial courses and A-level economics. There is some concern being expressed by the staff as they feel the department is losing its identity and being absorbed by technology.

History

This area received a lot of input in terms of staff development and new materials in preparation for the national curriculum. However, the need for fieldwork is putting a strain on resources. There are insufficient books in the library when pupils wish to research some of the periods which were not covered in the previous schemes of work.

Geography

This area also received an injection of resources and staff development opportunities were increased in order to implement the national curriculum. The youngest member of staff is very keen to develop meteorology and feels that high quality facilities would attract pupils to the school. Others in the department would be against this specialised use of resources and feel that there are other priorities such as a field centre and computers in each classroom.

Art

Pupils work with enthusiasm in this area and several move on to take foundation courses with a view to a career in art and design. The space for art teaching is adequate and the condition of the decoration is of little concern because the walls are covered with pupils' work. However, the doors urgently need painting. The school has always had a good reputation for its pottery but one of the kilns is out of use because the finance committee was unaware of these particular pieces of equipment and had not budgeted for their maintenance. Fortunately, when a major problem arose it was near the end of the year so the staff managed with one kiln.

Music

The school staff who reviewed this area felt that there were no problems and no particular resource or development needs other than the purchase of large amounts of sheet music. The headteacher sought the advice of the LEA's music adviser and also of one of the parent governors. It would appear that a lot of curriculum and staff development is required. The head of music has now refused to organise any musical activities which fall outside his 1,265 hours.

Physical education

The departmental staff are working hard to introduce the national curriculum's programmes of study on time. They are attending courses at the local polytechnic and are organising after-school workshops. It is becoming increasingly difficult to find enough schools who are willing to take part in Saturday morning sporting activities. There are more after-school fixtures but these always seem to involve a lot of rushing around to arrive on time. The head of department is looking into the possibility of obtaining fixtures against independent schools. The governors seem unaware of the long-term financial implications of the swimming pool. Current maintenance programmes will result in the need for major expenditure in a few years' time. It may be possible to increase the income from the pool as it is used very little outside school hours. The surface of the tennis courts is beginning to break up and further frost damage could make the courts too dangerous to use.

RE

Each class has a weekly period of RE and there is an agreed syllabus.

Cross-curricular themes

The cross-curricular themes coordinator works with heads of department and the deputy head (academic) to ensure that the requirements of the national curriculum are being considered and that an incremental approach is used to introduce change.

Information technology is considered to be integral to all subjects although specific emphasis is placed on the use of wordprocessing in English, databases in history, and spreadsheets in mathematics and science. However, most staff feel that the centralisation of the computers and printers in the IT suite does not facilitate genuine cross-curricular use.

Environmental education an audit is currently under way to establish the extent to which this is covered across the curriculum.

Citizenship a report on the coverage of this theme is planned to take place soon.

Economic and industrial understanding is covered during technology lessons and projects in Years 7 and 8. It is developed through an industry day for Year 9 during which the pupils take part in simulated industrial problems in order to develop their abilities to build and work in teams and to solve problems. This experience is followed up by an enterprise week in Year 10 as well as work experience and careers education and guidance in Years 10 and 11.

Health Education is well established and is covered by personal and social education, and by PE.

Special needs

The learning development department tests all pupils on entry to the school. The head of this department meets with primary school staff to discuss the needs of pupils who have specific learning difficulties, those who are very weak academically and those identified as very gifted. Most of the work with these pupils is done by supporting normal timetabled lessons but some withdrawal of pupils (e.g. during registration periods) takes place. Clubs and residential courses are organised for groups of pupils with special needs (e.g. a residential cross-curricular course to Derbyshire is organised for very able pupils in Year 8). The progress of all special needs pupils is monitored by the head of learning development and the deputy head (pastoral). A 'special needs' group of staff meets twice a term and has a representative from each department. It provides a forum for discussion of teaching and learning strategies and the list of pupils needing special help is regularly reviewed. A few pupils are 'statemented' and have additional support.

Sixth form

The school has a relatively traditional sixth form (Years 12 and 13) comprising 54 pupils in the lower sixth and 45 pupils in the upper sixth. The courses offered are:

- Two year A-level courses in English, mathematics, history, geography, physics, chemistry, biology, design, home economics, French, German, government and politics, economics, music, art, theatre studies;
- Secretarial course which lasts up to two years;
- GCSE (and equivalent) courses (which may be combined with A-levels or the secretarial course) in computer literacy and information technology, electronics, English, environmental science, geology, mathematics, media studies, photography, physical education, sociology, travel and tourism, vehicle design.

In addition, pupils may, by negotiation, retake GCSEs with individual tuition from subject staff.

The sixth form curriculum also includes general studies (which incorporates a religious education input) and the suspension of the normal timetable for theme days and for activities week (which includes work-shadowing and higher education talks/visits). Informal market research by the head of sixth form among current Year 10 and 11 indicates that some students may go to the local FE college for A-levels because it offers psychology. There is also pressure from many directions to introduce more vocational programmes.

2.   Human resources

The school currently has a well established staff of 54 full-time equivalent teachers including the headteacher. The headteacher was appointed in 1978 and is expected to retire in August 1993. The deputy head (academic) has been in post for ten years and has indicated his intention to retire with the head. The other two deputies were appointed two and three years ago.

Many of the staff are young and ambitious. It is clear that they will seek promotion, either within the school or outside. It is important to provide them with development opportunities and to involve them in decision-making. Half the staff will take part in the appraisal process during 1992–93 and the rest in 1993–94. This should allow them to express their career and development aspirations.

The support staff in some areas are rather confused about the exact limits of their responsibilities. None of the teaching or non-teaching staff has a job description so these need to be developed alongside the appraisal process.

The governors do not have a pay policy but some of the newer members of the governing body are keen to link this to the outcomes of appraisal.

There is a feeling amongst governors that some have a lot more decision-making power than others. However, it is generally felt that governor and senior management team roles and relationships should be reconsidered when the new headteacher is in post.

3.   Pupil welfare and pastoral care

A deputy head, working with the heads of year, is responsible for this element. There is no formal pastoral curriculum so form tutors determine the activities which are carried out while they are with the pupils. For the formal academic subjects, Years 7 and 8 are taught in mixed ability groups based on tutor groups. Years 9, 10 and 11 are taught in mixed ability classes based on tutor groups for games, PE, PSE and RE. For the other subjects the timetable is blocked so that subject staff can decide whether to set, band or have mixed ability groups.

The school was part of the local authority's pilot scheme for the introduction of positive discipline policies. The policy was developed with the involvement of all staff and it is now being implemented. The equal opportunities policy was developed in 1988. It has proved a useful framework within which to operate but there have been cases, amongst both the staff and the pupils, which have demonstrated that the policy needs reviewing and reinforcing.

A brief academic report is completed in the Spring term by subject staff so that pupil progress can be closely monitored; the report and record of action taken is passed on to parents. Parents receive a full written report in the Summer term and are invited to parent/subject teacher evenings held during the year. Parents are welcome to contact the school at any time to discuss the progress of their children.

The school has developed some links with the main feeder primary schools so that progress through the attainment targets of the national curriculum can be monitored. It is hoped that, in the future, there can be greater co-operation with the rural schools and with those who only send a few pupils as only the head of special needs has made real links there.

Stronger two-way relationships could be formed with some of the major employers in the area. At the moment, work experience is seen in isolation from the rest of the curriculum.

The LEA intends to devolve funding for many of its support services from April 1994. The school needs to audit the extent to which it uses such services.

4. Physical resources

The school was built on a traditional pattern, and in addition to many individual classrooms there is a wide range of specialist rooms. Recent changes in the structure of the curriculum and in approaches to teaching and learning have resulted in the need to reconsider the physical provision, although in general it is still appropriate. Much of the school's furniture was new ten years ago with the exception of computing and technology which is five years old. There needs to be a forward plan for replacement. Routine maintenance is carried out by local contractors and seems to be running smoothly. Part of the internal fabric of the school was redecorated four years ago, and there needs to be a rolling programme of redecoration.

The entrance hall has been redecorated but it needs to be made more welcoming. The pictures are old and there is nowhere for visitors to sit. In addition, this tends to be the place where deliveries are left and where pupils wait to be disciplined by a deputy head.

Externally, some areas need attention:

(a)   The direction signs from the gate to the school entrance are dilapidated;
(b)   The low brick walling alongside the drive is beginning to look dangerous; and
(c)   The tarmac on the tennis courts has some holes in it.

There is a need for greater clarity concerning the school's areas of responsibility and those of the LEA. The chair of governors has heard conflicting stories from some schools.

5.   Pupil roll and marketing

The school has 816 pupils in the 1991–92 school year, divided as follows:

Year	7	8	9	10	11	12	13
Pupils	124	139	154	153	147	54	45

An important aim is to return to pupil numbers around 150 a year (five form entry) in order to guarantee the viability which comes from economies of scale. Even if this is achieved quite quickly, there will still be problems as the present Year 7 and 8 move through the school.

There is considerable significance in the fact that older pupils bring different amounts of money to the school. It can be very cost effective to recruit a few more sixth form students who can fit into existing A-level groups as the cost of providing for them is marginal. The provision of more vocational courses should attract pupils but there could be high costs in terms of personnel, equipment and materials.

The school has a new prospectus but plans for marketing are rather *ad hoc*. There is not, currently, an established 'marketing group' to organise a coordinated approach in this area. Improvements to the entrance hall and to communications with the school office appear to be necessary. However, a whole school approach to marketing is needed.

6. Management structures and approaches

The school's senior management team comprises the headteacher, three deputies and the head of sixth form. The deputy head (academic) leads the heads of department in curriculum development; the deputy head (pastoral) leads the heads of year in the maintenance of an effective system of pupil welfare and pastoral care. The third deputy is responsible for administration. The support staff are managed by a recently appointed bursar. There is a need to clarify roles and then to build teams which will be able to take on a greater responsibility for management.

There is a need to examine the effectiveness of internal and external communications as there have been several examples of misunderstandings in the past year. Already the office staff have asked for an answering machine to take calls out of hours and for a fax machine for speedy communications. The head of the sixth form has commented on how valuable these would be in the period around A-level results day in dealing with admissions tutors.

There is a need to make more use of the computerised management information system at strategic, tactical and operational levels. Its more widespread use will have implications for hardware and for staff development.

7. Monitoring and evaluation mechanisms

The monitoring of pupil progress through assessment is seen to be an integral part of the teaching and learning in the school. The formative, summative, informative, and evaluative nature of assessment are recognised and incorporated into school policy. Formal tests are held regularly within most departments and each year group has an annual test week, the results of which are reported to parents. There is a need for all departments to examine the ways in which they respond to test results in order to inform curricular programmes for individual pupils.

Departments must be helped to develop the skills of self-evaluation in order to give teachers ownership of the changes which are required. The governors have stated their intention to introduce a formal system of whole school evaluation or inspection, possibly every five years. The introduction of this would need very careful management.

8.   Financial resources

During the last financial year the school had a surplus of around £3,000. Monitoring suggests that this year's spending may result in a slight deficit.

In order to calculate much of the income to the school, the LEA weights pupils according to age based entirely on the previous January's Form 7. The age weighted pupil units are thus calculated as follows:

Pupil age at 31/8	Weighting
18+	2.168
17	2.237
16	2.198
15	1.601
14	1.532
13	1.484
12	1.484
11	1.484

The predicted income for 1992–93 is just over £1.5 million. This will fall slightly in real terms in 1993–94 as larger and more 'lucrative' year groups leave the school. The exact financial implications of the anticipated pupil population over the next three to five years needs to be calculated.

There is virtually no income from lettings but this area could be investigated as part of an overall review of income potential. A sponsored walk can be held every three years and is capable of raising about £2,000–£3,000 if a specific target is identified. The Hodgkin Trust could be approached to provide funds for curricular materials and grants for individual pupils. The sixth form committee raises a levy on its own students and runs a tuck shop, using the funds as it sees fit. This has included refurbishment to the sixth form area.

The next chapter shows the way in which this information can be summarised to form a strategic overview with key action areas highlighted in the form of the school development plan report.

9   Grantwich High School — The development plan report

The senior management team has collected the detailed plan for each element and for each area of the curriculum in order to build up the whole school development plan. While the individual elements were being built up, there was a series of occasions when those responsible for each element could meet to discuss the direction of their development and could work with senior management to fulfil the overall school aims and objectives. Some governors were able to join planning groups and the rest were kept informed of developments through reports to the full meeting of the governing body. We show here the whole school report which was produced as a result of this process. Detailed plans for each element and for the curricular areas would be available on request and could follow the format of the Bexley report in Chapter Five.

Grantwich High School
Development plan for the academic year 1992–93

Section One: A profile of the school, including its aims

Grantwich High School is a comprehensive school for 11–18 year olds situated to the south of the town, adjoining open countryside.

Built in the 1930s the school enjoyed extensive renovation and expansion in 1977. Although structurally sound, the school is in need of some redecoration and refurbishment. The senior management team is currently preparing a report to regroup subject areas in specific parts of the school.

The current teaching staff establishment is a headteacher, three deputies and 50 full-time equivalents. The school is fortunate to have a well established and skilled team of support staff.

There are 816 pupils on roll. The school can accommodate a yearly roll of 150 pupils but at the moment entry is considerably less than this. Strategies are being developed to improve the school's reputation and its marketing effort.

The school has a policy of mixed ability teaching in the first two years with various forms of pupil grouping (including by ability) thereafter.

Good relationships are maintained with the feeder primary schools within the town and links are being established with primary schools over a wider geographical area.

In the past the local high technology industries have flourished and provided a range of work experience opportunities for pupils. However, several companies are affected by the recession so that these opportunities are declining. Similarly, the recession has also impacted on the employment prospects of school leavers but the number of pupils going on to higher education has continued to increase. The governors are considering broadening the range of post-16 provision in the light of national economic and educational trends.

Section Two: A summary of trends (internal and external)

The implementation of the national curriculum continues to dominate curriculum development although there is continuing uncertainty about the final shape of the curriculum, particularly at Key Stage 4. There are increasing pressures to introduce more vocational courses, especially post-16. Parent and pupil choice will be partly influenced by the curriculum offered. Central government is also focusing on test and examination results by which many parents are now judging schools. The school has been involved in extensive discussions in order to present parents with a more sophisticated analysis of pupil achievement than that which is available by using crude scores only.

Development of decentralised school management with the school taking increasing responsibility for its own budget will continue to absorb a considerable amount of senior management time. Central government, while retaining certain powers for itself, is seeking to locate more and more decision-making at the school level. For this to be effective, greater staff involvement and development will be necessary. It is difficult to maintain the quality of resources when the local economy is in recession and the LEA is threatened with penalties for overspending.

To meet the increasing requirements of the staff and to improve the quality of teacher performance, central government is imposing teacher appraisal processes on the school. In response to this, the school is developing its scheme within the broad guidelines suggested by the LEA. Although the devolution of responsibilities to the school and the introduction of appraisal will necessitate the definition of roles and responsibilities, it is likely that a new head will wish to examine structures and, perhaps, initiate change within the next three years.

There are plans for new housing within the catchment area but existing new developments are only selling very slowly so it is unlikely that there will be a noticeable effect on the pupil roll in the near future. The relocation of central government departments will definitely take place from 1993 to 1995. However, this will not necessarily affect the number of children living in Grantwich.

> **Section Three:**   A central plan giving medium-term developments

Effective education for pupils depends on having a highly motivated staff. All teaching staff will be appraised over the next two years so as to identify their development needs and their career aspirations. Job descriptions will be drawn up for all staff and this will give a focus to subsequent appraisal discussions. The governors feel that they should move towards a system of performance related pay over the next three or four years, although many of the teaching staff would see this as divisive. It is clear that some form of pay policy will need to be developed. The devolution of responsibilities to the school from the LEA has meant that senior managers are overburdened. This role overload should be reduced and the job satisfaction of other staff should be increased by further devolution of responsibilities to a variety of teams within the school. However, the change must be carefully managed and the appropriate staff development, including team building, must be provided. It is expected that the new head will be appointed in the Spring of 1993 and that he or she will review the roles of the senior management team.

A marketing strategy is needed if the school is to flourish in the more competitive market. A group needs to investigate the best way of managing the school's reputation but it is clear that certain issues must be tackled quickly. The educational product is of a high quality but that fact must be reinforced both within and outside the school. There needs to be attention paid to the appearance of the premises and to the quality and siting of equipment for effective curriculum delivery. The development of new sixth form courses and the improvement of links with primary schools should increase numbers at both ends of the school.

Curriculum development is always taking place although the scale and pace of change should be carefully considered in order to avoid innovation overload and an ineffective education for the pupils. The integration of information technology into the classroom and into the school's management processes has implications for the provision of hardware and for access to software. It is intended that reviews of provision should include a large number of non-specialist users, whereas previous plans have always been drawn up by the computing specialist. The governors wish to see a thorough review of each area of the curriculum on a rotating basis and a whole school review or inspection every five years.

> ***Section Four:*** An action plan for the coming year

The plans for each of the core and support elements and for the curricular areas are available on request from any of the school's deputy heads. The whole school action plan is shown here (as Figure 9.1) in order to summarise the main areas to be covered in the next three years. This plan also indicates timing and success criteria for each of the tasks to be tackled over the next academic year.

Grantwich High School

Whole school plan —

(schematic diagram)

Figure   9.1

Figure 9.1   **SCHOOL MANAGEMENT DEVELOPMENT PLAN:**

WHOLE SCHOOL PLAN	YEAR 1 (1992–93)	YEAR 2 (1993–94)
CURRICULUM and CURRICULUM DEVELOPMENT	1. Examine decentralised IT provision 2. Review library provision 3. Inspect music curriculum 4. Investigate potential of vocational 6th 5. Cross-curricular themes ———————▶—	1. Implement decentralised IT policy 2. Evaluate work of English dept 3. Assess second language provision
HUMAN RESOURCES	1. Negotiate job descriptions 2. Introduce appraisal 3. Provide management development course 4. Succession planning for headteacher	1. Implement job descriptions 2. Continue appraisal programme 3. Decentralise decision making 4. New head and deputy in post
PUPIL WELFARE PASTORAL CARE	1. Build links with rural primary feeder schools 2. Review pastoral curriculum 3. Cost use of support services from LEA	1. Review equal opportunities policy 2. Examine success of primary/secondary transfer
PHYSICAL RESOURCES	1. Reorganise entrance hall 2. Replace signs and drive wall 3. Replace art kilns	1. Review maintenance of pool 2. Resurface tennis courts 3. Begin rolling programme of — redecoration and refurbishment
PUPIL ROLL and MARKETING	Target: Roll [808] Year 7 intake [130] 1. Establish marketing group 2. Evaluate 6th form position	Target: Roll [815] Year 7 intake [146] 1. Marketing plan implemented— 2. New 6th form courses
MANAGEMENT STRUCTURES and APPROACHES	1. Review communications in school 2. Build teams 3. Review use of MIS	1. Review external communications 2. Decentralise decision-making 3. Develop MIS as management tool
MONITORING and EVALUATION MECHANISMS	1. Establish monitoring and evaluation parameters and criteria	1. Staff development on self-evaluation of areas of the school 2. Establish and introduce performance indicators
FINANCIAL RESOURCES	1. Forward planning: income and expenditure 2. Investigate lettings 3. Improve budgetary information	1. Utilise trust fund money 2. Implement lettings policy 3. Investigate cost of field centre 4. Review contracts

GRANTWICH HIGH SCHOOL

YEAR 3 (1994-95)	YEAR 1 (1992–93)	
	TIME TARGETS (including cycle of governors' meetings)	SUCCESS CRITERIA Performance indicators
1. Review decentralised IT and the support for it 2. Evaluate work of the maths department	1. All year 2. Autumn 3. Spring 4. Autumn 5. All Year	1. Policy statement 2. Action plan 3. Inspection report 4. Action plan 5. Effective provision
1. Evaluate teacher performance 2. Investigate performance related pay 3. Review relationships with governors	1. Autumn/Spring 2. September 3. All Year 4. Immediate	1. Agreed statements 2. 50% staff involved 3. 25% of middle managers 4. New head in place
1. Review positive discipline policy 2. Review mixed ability teaching	1. Autumn 2. Spring 3. Summer	1. Number of contacts 2. New policy 3. Costings
1. Review major equipment maintenance and replacement	1. Spring 2. Autumn 3. Autumn	1. Pleasant environment 2. New signs and wall repair 3. New kiln
Target: Roll [823] Year 7 intake [150] 2. Increased size upper 6th	1. April 2. January	1. Marketing plan 2. New structure
1. Review senior management roles and responsibilities 2. Review relationships with governors	1. Summer 2. Easter 3. Summer	1. Report and action plan 2. Training complete 3. Evaluation report
1. Whole school evaluation 2. Governors compile evaluation report	1. All Year	1. Criteria established
1. Review lettings policy 2. Cost implications of performance related pay and develop pay policy	1. April 2. Summer 3. December	1. Five year plan 2. Policy agreed 3. New monitoring statement

10 Conclusion

This book has set out to analyse the nature and dimensions of school development planning and to provide a practical framework for schools to evaluate their planning processes. The importance of school development planning for self-managing schools cannot be overemphasised. The considerable powers that schools have received with the decentralisation of decision-making has significantly increased the burden on management in schools to plan, deliver and evaluate their activities. To do this in a coherent and effective way it is vital that schools not only produce a development plan but also mechanisms to evaluate the extent to which plans have been fulfilled.

It should, however, be emphasised that school development planning is not a 'one off' activity but a rolling programme where plans are constantly adjusted to meet changing circumstances.

What follows is a series of key points that schools can reflect upon to assess their process to date:

- **Those who don't plan plan to fail** — management should be proactive rather than reactive, thus for a school to be able to take the initiative and control its own future, strategic planning is a vital activity;

- **It is important to consider the process** — by which the plan is to be built up because involvement in the decision-making process will help to ensure that the product i.e. the plans are actually put into practice;

- **Plans should be available** — and open to anyone who wishes to see them as well as to those who will use them, either to inform activities or as a monitoring scheme;

- **Plans should be user friendly** — so that all readers find them informative and relevant;

- **Plans should be brief, strategic and to the point** — so that major developments can be isolated; activity focused and the reader is not drowned in a sea of detail;

- **Plans should be written for use by the school** — not merely to conform to an LEA blueprint;

- **Plans should be seen to be a working document** — not put away in a drawer to be brought out once a year;

- **Plans should be adaptable, flexible documents** — not seen as 'cast in tablets of stone' but responsive to changed circumstances.

Concluding remarks

Schools have faced an increasing number of initiatives from central government over the last few years. Coping with the volume and complexity of this change is both a daunting and exhausting task. This has often led schools into coping with the change on a day-to-day basis in the hope of surviving to cope with the next onslaught! If the quality of education that we are able to offer to our children is to improve it is vital that a clear education vision is set down and effective means are put forward to achieve that vision. The only coherent way of achieving this is for a school to engage in a meaningful process of school development planning to set a course through the changing sea of educational provision. We hope this book has provided some help on that journey.

Index